The Leader with Seven Faces

The Leader
with
Seven Faces

Finding your own ways to
practice leadership
in today's organization

Leandro Herrero

First published in 2006 by:
Meetingminds Publishing
An imprint of The Chalfont Project Ltd
PO Box 1192, Beaconsfield, Bucks, HP9 1YQ, United Kingdom
www.meetingminds.com

ISBN-10 Paperback: 1-905776-00-4
ISBN-13 Paperback: 978-1-905776-00-9

Printed and bound in the United Kingdom

A CIP catalogue record for this title is available from the British Library

This book is dedicated to Carrie.

It has been inspired by my work with clients, my experiences with great leaders (and toxic leaders!) and my own memories as leader of business organizations for more than fifteen years.

It is also dedicated to leaders who don't make business headlines, haven't climbed the Himalaya, haven't crossed the Atlantic solo, haven't fought a war or haven't been the subject of a case study in a business school. They simply give the best of themselves in everyday life and take others with them on different quests. Many of them may not even recognize the title of leader, but the wellbeing, welfare and growth of others depend for a great part on them.

Finally, it is written in memory of my tired father, who is now resting forever. He would have never considered himself a leader during his life in front of a textile machine, but people who depended on him at that old factory respected and loved him.

Contents

What you say
Speak
Meaning
Intention

What you do
Role model
Change
Practice 7 Faces

Where you go
Maps
Destinations
Journeys

THE LEADER
WITH
SEVEN
FACES ©

What you are
Awareness
Responsibility
Identity

What you build
Space & Time
Homes
Legacy

How you do it
Drivers
Styles
Structures

What you care about
Values
'The system'
Non-negotiable

Introduction
Not another book on leadership!

Well, yes, another one! And I suspect it won't be the last one either. But I want to believe that this is a different one. This is mainly a long conversation with yourself, with me, perhaps with others. It is also based upon a novel idea: let's find out what the questions are before giving answers. A second unusual idea: I used plain English as much as I could !

I don't know you and I don't know where you are. Where you spend your working life. Perhaps as leader in a corporation, or in an NGO, or in government, or in education, or the Church, or a religious institution. In the private or the public sector. All I know is that you are reading this and something somewhere must have made you do it.

What an intriguing issue. Academics, practitioners, consultants, self-help gurus, generals, priests, rabbis, imams, political leaders and community workers are romancing, framing, developing and playing with the idea of leadership. It has been happening for a long, long time. The leadership shop is big. The bookshelves are full.

We have a wealth of surveys and data, categories and taxonomies, lists of leadership competences and styles. We have case studies and biographies, confessions of success and failure, supporters of charisma and supporters of an almost

1

invisible leadership. We seem to have more information, knowledge and stories on the subject than we can handle. So, why does it still feel as if we know nothing about leadership?

Business school frameworks and executive development programmes tend to look at this from a rather short-sighted modern world perspective. Yes, philosophy, history and literature have always addressed leadership in one form or another. But the business and organizational world is still impermeable to anything outside their traditional borders. Seeing things from the perspective of the 21st century organization, the latest 'framework' and the latest 'research findings', it all seems novel, cute, well-labelled, blessed by the brand of any well-known guru and elevated to gospel by the names of 'the experts'. But we are kidding ourselves with the pretended novelty of many modern classifications of leadership or ... of anything, for that matter. *"There is nothing new under the sun"*, as the Greeks said. But the modern world, the post-modern world and the post-9/11 one (it is impossible to avoid this punctuation in history) all struggle with learning from the past *and* with not getting too hooked on it. It's a moving target. Past or present? Constantine or Jack Welch? Just kidding.

▶ *Leadership for all seasons?*

Leadership as a topic is ranked higher than ever in the list of things to pay attention to, whether this is in a business organization, an NGO, a political party, the Churches, or any association of human beings trying to make sense of the future. From institutions such as the UN to initiatives such as fighting AIDS: the question of leadership is hot. And yet, it is sometimes difficult to know what exactly people are talking about.

This business of 'leadership' seems and feels both old and new, easy and difficult, 'big thing' and trivialized at the airport bookstore. We are trying to capture a fascinating phenomenon, and, frankly, any help, 'map', study and framework is welcome. But if you are looking for the *definitive* method and the *final* unquestionable ten-laws-of, you have a problem. Just think for a second. We are trying to understand something that has been attributed to Mother Theresa, Sir Richard Branson, Hitler, Bill Gates, Churchill, Gandhi, Jack Welch, Khmer Rouge's Pol Pot, Tony Blair and Jonny Garcia. Yes, all of them.

What? You don't know who Jonny Garcia is? Me neither, because he is somebody who has never made headlines. He works as a field community worker in a remote area of a remote country and, believe me, judging by the hundreds of people who follow him, admire him, would die for him and count on him, he is a great leader. We just don't know him. He is invisible to us.

▶ *Models and caricatures*

The 'example of' (leadership) territory is also a curious one. There is a plethora of books taking the life of any public figure and recommending it for 'leadership thinking'. One used to have to wait until people were dead, won a war or liberated a country, but apparently now all that is needed, is that they are out-of-office or just a public figure/role-model/global entertainer (and those borders are getting blurred.) So, in the airport bookstore, leadership à la Colin Powell (the military has always been a good factory of these) rubs shoulders with leadership à la Mandela, à la Thatcher and à la Bush. Other shelf-companions range from football players to Formula-1 racers and round-the-world-solo-sailors. I can't comment on the latter, because the combination of leadership and sport has always interested me as much as the history of 18th century farming in New Zealand. Apologies for the bias.

Seriously, what do all these people have that justifies grouping them under one single universal adjective: Leader? What is it? Would it perhaps be worth pulling all those 'lives' together, detailing all qualities and attributes of these publicly-declared leaders, entering them into the-mother-of-all-mathematical-analysis and hoping that a printout would give us 'the answer'? Well, it has been tried. Not always using maths, but certainly through hundreds - if not thousands - of biographies and meta-biographies. The result? A rich supermarket of traits, qualities, attitudes, behaviours and 'examples of'.

Do you want them? Do you fancy guidelines, mirrors, inspirations? No problem. The Big Supermarket of Leadership literature, leadership development and leadership training has it. When you put together all the attributes that have been 'found' or have been proven successful for leaders, you quickly reach a conclusion: short of walking on water (and only Moses came close to that, only surpassed by Jesus Christ himself), anything goes. So those lists are only of relative help.

We are told that leaders have integrity, enthusiasm, resilience, fairness, humility, warmth and confidence, to quote a well-respected 'study'. So, if you are an integral, warm, resilient, humble, fair and confident chap, does that make you a leader? Or do leaders share those attributes with non-leaders? And if so, what's all the fuss about the ('research') list?

To 'elevate this confusion to a higher level', it would probably also be safe to say that what has worked in one place, may not necessarily work in another. Similarly, that what has worked before, may not work now. Pretty gloomy conclusion for those who love a predictable world.

But let's be a bit kinder. Is there really anything wrong with that rich supermarket of findings on qualities, attributes or behaviours? Not really. They serve good conversation and possibly inspiration. But it doesn't quite solve the problem of YOU or ME becoming a leader. Because - and I'm speaking for myself here - I don't have the flamboyant entrepreneurship cum exhibitionism of a Richard Branson, I am not leading a country to independence dressed in a handkerchief, I can't craft those Churchillean speeches, I am definitely not running General Electric and clearly - believe me! - I am no Mother Theresa either.

So, it is not worth 'studying' all these people, right? The answer to that question varies: no, yes and maybe. I have just said that any help is welcome. Looking at what these 'big leaders' do or have done, may be helpful if the result is a trigger for reflection and maybe an inspiration for a translation into our more mundane life. It's not helpful if the result is to put you off forever. Let me explain. If you are fascinated by the so-called charisma of Richard Branson and believe that he truly represents your ideal leader, you may decide to call it a day if you think that your genes would never allow for any Bransonian extravaganza. If you are at some level of managerial responsibility in an organization and admire the brilliance of the rhetoric of 'Somebody-Leader', but you feel you are not the verbal type, you may decide that your progression in the organization is limited. And so on. In my professional career, I have seen many people - more than I expected - giving up on the idea of 'the leadership thing' because of the association of the concept with the grandiose, the great and the CEOs. And therefore, it was not for them.

I believe that to look at all those 'examples of leadership' is helpful, but only if you are able to rise above the images, the ideas, the leadership programmes, the names and their lives, the surveys, the checklists of attributes, the sets of qualities and look yourself in the mirror and ask the question: *"OK, why not? I'm no Branson, no Gandhi, no Welch, but I can be a pretty good leader if..."*

Right, we have found the 'if'.

Let me introduce you to this book by sharing its premises:

[1] What's leadership?
This is my definition. It is the ability to exercise meaningful influence on others who voluntarily accept it, leaving behind a visible legacy of collective impact.

These keywords are relevant:

- **Influence:** it may be translated in different forms: inspiration, reflection, sense of meaning, direction or, very possibly (but not necessarily and/or not always apparent), action!

- **Meaningful:** I am assuming some magnitude or substantial degree, a directional change, a lasting impact, almost even, dare I say, teleological. I mean the provision of big-time meaning and purpose, not the short term ephemeral impact.

- **Others:** the old definition of 'leader' (i.e. the one who has a follower) has not yet been matched by any academic!

- **Voluntarily:** I am sorry, but it is not good enough that somebody has been declared my leader. Unless I accept it, there is no real leader. There may be an official party leader, team leader, executive leadership team or Supreme Leader, and I may even be resigned to using the terms <u>BUT</u> I am the only one who decides who my leader is. Let me expand on this. Leaders become, dictators arrive. Leadership is something that you earn, which means that there must be somebody giving it to you. That means there are followers. You can be my boss, my dictator, my inquisitor or my king by decree. But you can only be my leader when I say so and I ask you, and - incidentally - it would be nice if you accepted.

- **Legacy:** Here, a whole spectrum of possibilities applies: from the wonderful memories to the big mess. But it must be something that's left behind.

[2] To be or to become a leader or to enhance one's ability, you need to practice it.
To practice leadership, you need 'a map' and lots of questions. We are far from a shortage of answers – remember those shelves - but we're not sure we have the right questions. So we may just be kidding ourselves with sets of beautiful answers to the wrong questions. This book is mainly about questions, and:

- The answers to these questions are personal.
- Unfortunately, the consequences of your answers are not. Other people at work, home, party, church, organization or in the wider society depend on them. No pressure…

If after reading this or other books, attending my or other seminars, getting other help and other triggers, it is not obvious to you *what to practice*, I think you'll have a problem (if you still aspire to be or become a leader). Note that I say *what to practice*, not whom to emulate.

You'll know that you are a leader when others think of you in that way voluntarily. *"The proof of the pudding is in the eating"*, my fellow compatriot Miguel de Cervantes said around 1615. The proof of your leadership capabilities is in the response and nature of your followers.

[3] The 'praxis' of leadership has different faces.
The practice of leadership may be helped by recognizing that the difficulty in making sense of the plethora of 'examples' is not necessarily that it consists of a mix of heroes, villains, charlatans, moralists, dictators, saviours, psychopaths and

normal people. That mix is obviously an intellectual challenge in itself (!), because, if nothing else, it's difficult to have an uncontaminated and clinical view of it without attaching a judgement to each 'case'. The Mother Theresa case is good, the Hitler case is bad. Sure, but that won't take us far.

The real difficulty, however, is one of presentation. Leadership is polyhedral, pardon my language. You can be looking at one of the polygons and get excited about it, only to realize that there are others just as exciting on the other side of the three-dimensional solid.

Yes, the leader has seven faces. In some leaders, only one or two are visible. When those leaders are proposed as examples or role models, the only faces of leadership we see are the ones they show us. When you as leader are 'in front' of your people, perhaps one or two faces are visible. But there are others, equally important. These seven faces are:

- **What leaders say**. Rhetoric, language, words… matter. Many organizations are stuck on something (strategy, process improvement, change) because they do not posses 'another language'. Leaders provide 'language' and meaning, a framework in which action can take place. If this is their visible face, leaders look more like teachers and educators, and language and meaning become the most visible traits.

- **Where leaders go.** Leaders go places and take people with them. Some of them have a pretty good idea of the destination, perhaps too good an idea. Others are more of the type who 'enjoy the journey'. However, if this is the visible face, both look more like cartographers, explorers or conquistadores. Life around them inevitably revolves around these themes of destiny and pathways.

- **What leaders build.** Leaders are builders of organizations or 'projects'. They build purpose and they build places. Places to be, to enhance people, to work in, to think, to do, to succeed, to attract people, to navigate through life. They build other things such as trust and relationships. If this is their predominant face, they look more like architects. 'Space' and its sister 'Time' are favourite themes around them.

- **What leaders care about.** Finding this face of the leader is not difficult, because what they care about forms their language and behaviour. See what the leader says, observe what the leader does, see if it matches and you will discover the value system behind it! When this is the main visible face, these leaders may look more like moralists or teachers, even if they may not necessarily use the language of morality. But what this face shows is mainly beliefs. Beliefs seem to form everything else.

- **How leaders do it**. Worrying about how things happen is prominent in some leaders. Very often, the 'how' is seen in our culture as 'a detail' or 'a by-product'. But some leaders don't see it like that. The way of doing things matters to them and this is their most visible face. When this is the case, they look more like stage managers focusing on styles, ways, dynamics, and plots. 'Ways of doing' may kill good visions. These leaders know it and worry about 'the how' almost above everything else.

- **What they are.** This is a sometimes difficult face to understand. Perhaps the best way to do this, is to refer to famous lines from the Jewish text *The Ethics of the Fathers: "If you don't look after yourself, who will?"* First stop. It looks pretty selfish, but it's enormously healthy, because it's prompting non-dependence on others. *"If you only look after yourself, what are you?"* Second stop here. This is a powerful question. Note the 'what', not 'who'. *"What am I?"* is probably the most important question of our navigation system in the world. And third and last stop: *"If not now, when?"*

  Some leaders worry about the 'what-we-are' and, if this is their predominant face, they look like identity seekers, rather constantly referring to a sense of belonging. Sometimes they look like historians as well, because identity and belonging are above everything else, with one eye on the past and another on the future. Awareness of themselves and others, including emotions, is very visible in them.

- **What leaders do.** This behavioural face is always fascinating. It is often the most 'visible' and one that is easier to refer to, mainly to imitate. What leaders do - or don't do – matters; for some people more than anything else (i.e. what they say, or build, or think…). This 'action-face' is certainly enormously important and the engine of the building of other dimensions, such as reputation and trust. It is powerful, both in its building and its destroying potential. Some leaders seem to have great ability to generate action around them, often seen as the only relevant dimension for themselves and the organization behind them. When the emphasis is on the doing and the main visible face is action, leaders sometimes look like heroes, or company acrobats, pointing to outcomes and measurements.

▶ *Do you have to practice everything?*

Our face reflects our soul, our being. We are used to it! We see it in the mirror every day. We may like it or not (!), but we are certainly familiar with it! That leadership face that you or others see, probably *is/represents* your main zone of comfort. You may be a natural doer who tends to focus on where to go, and then goes there! If so, you may tend to dismiss questions of style, beliefs or even 'ways of doing'. You will be tempted to practice leadership with that face and that is the only one that others will see. Nothing wrong with that, but remember that other people may react better to other faces; for example, the one of language, or values, or identity. I don't know. You could be better off practicing leadership with other faces. You may discover your hidden ones in the process!

Don't stay in your comfort zone. Practice all faces if you can! Practicing leadership with seven faces is NOT about 'perfect' leadership. It is about being sensitive to a very complex reality, the one of your business organization, or your non-profit institution, or your church, or your political party. In this incredibly complex reality, what leaders say, where they go and take people, what they build, what they care about, how they do it, 'what' they are and what they really do, matters equally. The leader with seven faces is a leader for a future that has already started.

▶ *My subjective world*

When I decided to write this book, I had many choices in front of me. Let me explain why I chose this one. I am a psychiatrist through background and professional experience. I practiced Medicine for about fifteen years and then I joined senior management ranks in the pharmaceutical industry on both sides of the Atlantic. I spent another fifteen years or so working for three different companies until I co-founded The Chalfont Project Ltd, an organizational consulting firm that I lead. Like any other life - yours perhaps - it has been a rollercoaster ride. But I feel privileged.

It would not make sense to summarize my 'learning' in bullet-points like a report sent to your manager. But some things - semi-connected themes - have struck me time and time again along the way:

1) Human behaviour is incredibly complex. What a statement! Psychology and Psychiatry are trying hard to find clues for every 'why'. But each time they think they have achieved something, they come up with a label that frames the issue (abnormal behaviour, for example) and gives some sense of comfort. Practitioners then know what to do or not to do. This is good news for their comfort and often good news as well for the individual who needs help. But it is far form providing a deep insight and understanding of the individual. Management

(Sciences, studies and education) is no different but it is usually more superficial. We fabricate an enormous amount of things (frameworks, classifications, competence sets, checklists…) that help us navigate. But again, this is far from giving us a deep understanding of what is really going on inside the organization! Leadership as a concept is the same. We can put all the studies together, all the theories and classifications and all the lists of 'qualities' and who knows, we might have some sort of language. Less good news: we may still not get to the bottom of what leadership *is*.

2) Early in my pharmaceutical industry life - which I found fascinating at first and a world apart from medical practice - I began to wonder why some organizations seemed to succeed, attract people and mobilize internal energy and why others - very often similar in size and culture - looked pretty pathetic and hopeless. In hindsight, the question now seems less grandiose or original, but at the time it kept coming to my mind. It didn't take me a lot more time to realize that the quality of characters in the organizational zoo didn't seem to correlate with anything. I found uninspiring leaders running entire departments apparently well, and inspirational leaders in charge of a mess, which made one wonder if it had been created by them. The complexity and sophistication of processes and systems didn't ensure success either. Compared with the world I was coming from - clinical and academia - the 'industry' was a Rolls Royce in information management, for example. But exciting as this was, it didn't ensure success either.

3) Leadership was progressively climbing the ladder of my list of interests as a 'place to find the clue'. Throughout my working history, I have made some evolving observations:

   a) Over all these years, I have found very few good leaders. I have found many people in top positions for whom the single, recurrent, nagging question I have had is: "*How on earth did they get there?*" The worst, most dangerous leaders I have found are the ones who appeared honest, ethical, people-oriented, compassionate, value-driven and even overtly religious, and who turned out behaving like little bastards. Their danger lies in their unexpected behaviour. Some of these 'leaders' used what I will describe later on in this book as the 'It's-the-system-not-me' argument to justify their - in some cases plainly inhumane – actions.

   b) I am now convinced that leadership is a practice that benefits from repetitive action and may even inversely correlate with how much we talk about it or how we use the label!

   c) I am also convinced that all of us have the potential to be a leader, possibly in different degrees, and that we can 'go for it', armed with some convictions and the desire to achieve things.

Over the last five odd years, I have led leadership executive development programmes with my clients and have constantly learned from them. This book represents a 'stop-and-capture-it' and will no doubt evolve with further editions. But, as I said, I had choices. I could use a significant amount of bibliography and references for the great and good of academia and consulting, and give the next pages a pseudo-scientific-experienced-academic-management-consulting validation. I could quote and re-quote the gurus. I could contrast frameworks and theories. I could 'critically analyze' positions and premises. I could propose trends and mega-trends. I could do any or all of the above, or I could simply bypass all of this and get straight into sharing some thoughts and experiences, bringing all insights together and providing you with lots of questions for which - very often - I haven't found answers myself. And in the process invite you to come along to find the answers.

I have mentioned before that this book is mainly 'a book of questions'. My years of leadership experience, my three professional qualifications in both science and business, my three careers and my (greying) hair loss have taught me that there is one single, overriding, most important management question. Everything else is totally secondary. That question is: *"What's the question?"* I will refer to this again in one of the chapters.

The ability to ask questions is a sign of leadership maturity. The ability to provide answers is not. If each time we were about to jump into action - analyse a 1,000-page market research report, draw a product development plan, create a recruitment and retaining HR strategy, produce the PowerPoint package for the retreat or sign that big capital expenditure - we stopped and thought and asked the question: *"What's the question I am trying to answer?"*...if we could do that, we would jump a few years in our collective leadership evolution… If I were to propose one single management education recipe, this would be the one.

This is a long explanation to tell you that you will not find comprehensive bibliographies and many references to theories of leadership in this book. When I do some of the above, it will be minimal and relevant to the conversation.

How to read /use this book

Follow the order of the seven faces or start anywhere. It's your choice. In each of the faces there is a conversation about three themes. Why those themes? This is important as an understanding between you and me: I am not pretending to create a comprehensive list of themes for each of the faces. I am not objective with you, nor am I interested in being objective with you.

The themes are very subjective because I am sharing my best assets with you: my experience. I am not trying to convey to you that I am in the possession of the truth. I would like to invite you to consider those themes and associated questions as a starting point for your own discovery. In the process, you will come up with many other themes and questions. I finish each chapter with an initial list of questions to trigger new ones in you.

- Reflect upon them and see if there are others, not listed but triggered in you by the conversation.
- Attribute a value: Is that very relevant to me? Is it new? Is it old but still valid? Intriguing?

- Check your status – how are you doing on these?
- How are you going to cultivate that face of leadership?
- Create an action and a mechanism in order to - what else? - practice it!

There is also a simple graph at the end of each chapter/face called 'Action Map', which intends to host all these key questions. The ones inside the boxes in each of the chapters are simple starting points. These graphs look like this:

ACTION MAP
(some first pass questions)

	Me	**My organization**
Me	This is mainly 'me and me' talking. This box will have a lot to do with awareness of the theme, the issue, topic, etc.	Here is the place to describe your impact on the organization, on the themes of the face. This is 'as you see it', and therefore you create the relevant questions.
My organization	This is the place to map how the organization sees you as leader. You don't know until you ask! If you haven't asked, guess first and ask later.	This is the view of the organization itself on itself. The questions here are from the collective perspective of the group you lead or belong to.

Use the blank spaces to make notes! Write some thoughts, more questions, some answers, anything!

Other ways? Of course, there are. I'm sure I can leave it to your imagination! However, if you're strapped for inspiration, here are some suggestions:

- Read it as a team exercise. Block sixty minutes each month and bring your team together to discuss 'one face'. Read the chapter and debate it. Try to deal with 'the questions' and see if you can get some collective 'answers'.

- Take a personal approach. Read it in whatever order you want and try to make it the basis of a personal plan. Take notes, write in it, highlight, rewrite…

- If you are in some sort of coaching programme or leadership development, take this book along as your companion, as a map to progress and move forward.

Let's go!

The Leader with Seven Faces

What you say

Speak
Meaning
Intention

What you do
Role model
Change
Practice 7 Faces

Where you go
Maps
Destinations
Journeys

What you are
Awareness
Responsibility
Identity

What you build
Space & Time
Homes
Legacy

How you do it
Drivers
Styles
Structures

What you care about
Values
'The system'
Non-negotiable

The Leader with Seven Faces

1 What you say
Speak
Meaning
Intention

The limits of my language mean the limits of my world.
Ludwig Wittgenstein[1]

It's August 28, 1963. The place: Lincoln Memorial in Washington, DC. Martin Luther King, Jr. is addressing the multitude:

"I have a 350-page strategic plan that first gives us the situation analysis of our racial problems and then describes a ten-point strategic programme and a set of milestones to achieve the desired outcomes and deliverables of equality that will add value to our nation."

Just kidding. How does it sound? Not credible? Actually, what he said was:

"I have a dream that one day on the red hills of Georgia the sons of former slaves and the sons of former slave-owners will be able to sit down together at a table of brotherhood. (…) I

---

[1] Wittgenstein, Ludwig, 2001, *Tractatus Logico-Philosophicus*, Routledge, London

have a dream that one day every valley shall be exalted, every hill and mountain shall be made low, the rough places will be made plain, and the crooked places will be made straight, and the glory of the Lord shall be revealed, and all flesh shall see it together."

Is that better? Too much? I know. You are going to tell me that this is typical populist rhetoric and you just can't imagine your CEO or yourself addressing the annual shareholder meeting or your own department in `the dream language'. Ok, ok! But where are we these days in terms of 'leadership language'? What do we hear? What do we speak? Does it matter?

I'd like to explore three themes with you in this 'What you say' face of leadership:

- **Speak:** the style, the rhetoric, the lexicon... That wonderful, very visible face of the leader *expressing* things.
- **Meaning:** the *substance*, the content, the making of any sense. The 'translation' for people of perhaps a vision or a view of the world.
- **Intention:** the aims of the 'speak', the ability to influence or not, the *effects* of what you say.

Speak

Agreed. We are not Lutherkings. We don't have to be. But *how-we-say-what-we-say* matters. Look at our average business-speak. It is usually bland, clinical, factual, bullet-pointed, PowerPointed. Ronald D Laing - British psychiatrist who died in 1989 and who was the father of what under his influence became the so-called 'anti-psychiatric' movement - wrote in quasi-desperation:

"Gone is any sense of possible tragedy, of passion. Gone is any language of joy, delight, passion, sex, violence. The language is one of the boardroom."

The boardroom! The issue here is not whether or not you agree with the first part of the statement, let alone Laing's, to say the least, controversial contributions to society. It is his comparative reality: the language of the boardroom! That is: pretty boring, uninspiring and jargon-rich. Pretty much you and me, (sometimes) in the nine-to-five office. By five o'clock, all dead by firing-squad firing bullets – bullet points, that is. Hey! I have nothing against bullet points! You'll see a few of them in this book! I am against the bullet-point-*only*-world where everything is reduced to them to be managerially correct!

▶ Dreams or nightmares?

It sometimes seems as if there are not many dreams left. Declaring the vision of the organization in terms of superior competitive advantage and enhancement of market capabilities that maximize shareholder value is not a dream. It is a nightmare. Why is it that business organizations - even non-profit ones - seem to have lost the ability (if they ever had it) to talk in terms of normal emotions and use the language of everyday life? Maybe some people are motivated by the superior competitive advantage and enhancement of their company's market capabilities that maximize shareholder value, but the question is, should they be professionally treated? I could recommend a psychiatrist or two.

One of the big problems is that our language easily confuses metrics - and its surrogate indicators of success - with a company's vision. The rhetoric of the metrics has taken over. Earnings per share are a measure, not a goal, but this is what we talk about in the boardrooms of public companies. Governments talk about targets: from gas emissions to hospital waiting lists. CEOs talk about earnings per share. The language of the measure obscures the substance. No wonder overall inspiration in the workforce has gone down. Perhaps Laing was right: *"Gone is any sense..."*

Where are the compelling visions of today's enterprises, the invitations for the quest for greatness? I know, lost in word-permutating mission statements. Steve Jobs, when he was CEO at Apple, didn't say, *"Let's make beige boxes that can produce text and graphs, sit on office desks computing data and information, which can easily be translated into bottom-line results."* Actually, what he said was: *"Let's make a dent in the Universe!"* A dent in the Universe! This is bold, ambitious language closer to King's dream than to the return on capital invested.

How many times in your career have you been invited to make a dent in any universe? How many times in your career have *you* invited anybody to make a dent in any universe? We are suffering from an epidemic of IDD (Inspiration Deficit Disorder). Perhaps living in the `In Today's Calendar we Trust' society, we've lost a sense of destiny in our organizations. Many of them are largely paralysed by the impending merger, the impending severance package or the impending plastic surgery and skin reconstruction of the organization chart.

▶ One tape, two hours max, no video, no third party transcripts

Huston Smith - who has written and broadcast extensively on religions - studies the language of Jesus Christ in his lovely book *The world's religions* (Harper, 1999). He gives us three interesting insights.

First, in terms of 'volume', Jesus Christ could not compete today with the self-help, New Age, or socio-political authors. His words could easily be captured on a single tape. Not a programme of 30 cassettes, 3 videotapes, two booklets and an extra bonus of a glossary and a CD-Rom, which constitutes a typical 'follow-this-and-you'll-be-OK' self-help programme. Two hours at most. That's it. And no book. All he wrote was on the sand.

Second, his language was what Smith calls `gigantesque', including camels walking through needles' eyes. Third, his language was *invitational*: let's do that, come with me and so on. And it is this third element that I insist on discussing with my clients - leaders in organizations: how much of an invitational language do you use? Most of the time, not much I suspect.

We use a bullet-point statement, PowerPoint-declaration-language: these are the objectives, 1, 2, 3; this is what we have to do, these are our goals and critical success factors.

Next, another list. And another. That's it. There is no invitation there. I have analysed dozens of mission and vision statements from many organizations. Most of them could have been computer-generated. They contain statements, but no invitations. There is no "*let's do it*", "*come with me*", "*let's get together*", "*let's walk as a team*". It's as sexy as reading the telephone directory.

The field of 'inspirational messages' becomes confused with the one of 'motivational language'. Sometimes people hire what are called 'motivational speakers' for sales conventions or company retreats. These meetings are mainly designed to boost morale, to create a climax, to elevate adrenaline levels. That's OK, but a cynical friend of mine says that their use correlates with the inability of the home leaders to articulate a compelling message. They fall back on entertainment in the absence of their own inspiration. My friend is often unkind, often right and often both.

The reality is that if you can't find anything truly inspirational in your business - no matter how many climbers of Himalayan Mountains or trans-oceanic solitary sailors you bring to the post-dinner speech slot - you'll run a pretty insipid company.

In many pharmaceutical companies I know, for example, the language of mergers, bigger market share, so-called synergy of R&D, global critical mass and increase return on shareholder investment has replaced the language of quality of life, the mastering of disease, the generation of health and the quest for greater wellbeing. There are no dents in the universe; the only dent is the one in the market.

▶ *Dreams and goals*

Dreams are not goals and objectives. In some quarters, there is still the idea that the big vision of the company, translated into objectives, needs to be cascaded down to everybody in the organization in a form of a pristine, logical tree. The goals of my boss, a translation of his boss's goals, need to be divided into several goals for me, which then de facto become the critical success factors of my boss's goals - do you get it? So, once a year, the entire enterprise becomes a rational-looking web of goals and objectives in the strategic and business planning ritual. Give me a goal for the lowest level employee and I should be able to trace it back to the goals of the chairman, the theory goes.

Thousands of hours have been spent in corporate headquarters to make sure that everybody has guidelines for the web of goals, which eventually can be presented into a several-thousand-PowerPoint-slide thick binder of Goals and Objectives that can be used as a reference by managers. Unfortunately, the main use, however, of this thick binder sitting on the bookshelves of the office is often to contain all the magazines and papers that tend to fall from one end of the shelf. These binders are excellent bookends.

Assuming that one could rationalize and create that perfect web or cascade and that the exercise would be of some benefit, staff would be sharing goals and objectives but no dreams. I can share objectives, commit to actions and perform duties with the same life-transforming inspiration as the one needed to recite the telephone directory out loud. Or I can do so because my company and I have compatible dreams.

▶ Bipolar rhetoric

Language creates reality. A language of 'I' creates an 'I-reality', an exclusive one. A language of 'We' creates a collective dream; it's a language of inclusiveness. You can choose to speak any leadership language you want. There are languages of innovation, of future, of numbers, of zero-defects, of customers, of greater-goods, of market share, of reflection, of action, of anger and resentment, of victory, of martyrdom, of misery, of joy, of invitation, of cold facts, of transformation of life, dents in universes, month-end-numbers, sales targets, saving lives, competition, war, collaboration, community, Darwinian survival, love, etc. The choice is yours. But be careful what language you speak, you may get exactly that kind of organization.

Language is powerful. Powerful-good and powerful-bad. Language has the ability to polarize social relationships. And today, the world has become more and more bipolar. Perhaps it has been a long hidden progression for many years, but the post-9/11 world is certainly one of bipolar rhetoric. It is not just 'you are with us or against us' - a choice that, as one US journalist pointed out during the immediate aftermath, people don't want, need or should have to make. The issue is how the space in the overall spectrum of thinking became occupied by the extremes. Being anti-war became anti-American or pro-terrorism. Suggesting that the hijackers were anything but cowards (a term that President Bush first used to describe them) became conspiracy. To explore the underlying causes of the atrocity became collusion with terrorism. Challenging the statement that 'they' had done it because "*they hate our values*", became sharing the terrorist's own values. I can understand how it happened, but this polarization is not good for our children's future! Words may end up being the real source of terror.

▶ War on words

And central to all the post-9/11 events are words. A war of words. The use of the term 'war' (on terror) is in itself legitimate to some, dangerous and inaccurate to others. The French prime minister at the time was quick to insist: "*We are not at war*". The term 'crusade' was quickly abandoned. There were discussions on the different meaning of 'terrorists' and 'freedom fighters'. And there was a late realization that 'Infinite Justice' - the original name of the then proposed military operation – offended those who see this as the patrimony of God alone. Worryingly, a vast paraphernalia of euphemisms - used in the past to describe the disappearance of people, groups or entire states as a potential consequence of military retaliation - returned. This was typified by the reappearance of an old war euphemism, 'collateral damage', to refer to civilian casualties. The release date of a Hollywood film with this name was postponed. Then, since it supposedly was 'civilization' that had been attacked, the discussions about what *civilization* means followed as well! For some there is one civilization; for others several - western, Islam, etc. Some referred to 'mankind' or 'humanity', others to 'civilization', many mixed and confused both.

Language, and nothing else, was the protagonist in the immediate post-9/11 time, and it hasn't left central stage since. Language is neither neutral nor universally understood. For most people, the West's post-9/11 lexicon and rhetoric response was composed, calm, and measured. For others, terribly dangerous. Both heard the same discourse!

The only unequivocal use of language that I heard around that time came from Bill Clinton who declared that, during his presidency, he had authorised the killing of the main terrorist suspect. Hey, this is clear, not catch and bring to justice, not take him to a court of law, but kill him. Many people were quick to stress that this does not go well with the concept of justice and democracy. But nobody could accuse the US ex-president of fiddling with rhetoric.

▶ The tyranny of the 'or'

A bimodal world is not entirely new now, but post-9/11 rhetoric certainly amplified it. Perhaps this is the way most of us think. After all, business life is full of bimodal thinking as well. We have been taught to choose between extremes. Nobody has put it better than Collins and Porras in their acclaimed book *Built to Last* (Harper Collins, 2004). The authors suggest that companies have a choice: to surrender to what they call 'the tyranny of the or' or to embrace the 'and'. Traditional strategy teaching tells us: you can't have it both ways, it is either A or B. Choose!

An example of this 'tyranny of the or' is often seen in traditional product development. The choice, for example, is supposedly between speed or quality. It is the belief that speed compromises quality. This automatically infers that doing things to a high quality must be slow. The problem is not in this apparently innocuous dichotomy, but in its pervasive power. One starts by acknowledging the choice and ends up de facto ensuring that anything fast is sloppy and any good quality document needs 20 people to sign it off. Bipolar thinking is powerful and dangerous: not just in the political arena, but also in pure and simple daily organizational life.

Why is this categorical, A or B, approach to reality so popular? I am convinced that it has to do with our way of dealing with uncertainty. If we are able to categorize quickly into 'boxes' - A or B, pro-western or pro-terrorism, shareholder value driven or socialist, manager or leader - our level of anxiety decreases and we can grasp and contain an otherwise complex reality. Categorization into a bimodal world is the best mind anxiolitic that our brain produces. Bipolarization is the Valium of the mind.

► Unspeak

Steven Poole's book *Unspeak* (Little, Brown & Company, 2006) is a clever laboratory of ideas on the use of language, particularly in political life. It examines the influencing and pervasive nature of terms such as 'terrorist', 'insurgent', 'enemy combatants', 'extremism' etc. How we call things, situations, bits of reality, matters. This is no news. But the use of different terms shapes a different reality. Since socio-political life is rich in what has been called 'language manipulation', unspeak examples are mainly to be found in this arena and Poole's book is full of them.

Today's political scepticism is often expressed in terms, "*it's all spin*". That is, nothing is what it seems anymore, it's all massaged, dressed up, sexed up, cooked and manipulated so that people are tricked and influenced. There is no society, only audience. In organizational terms: no organization, just another Town Hall meeting. Unspeak is sometimes developed in a hidden and perhaps unconscious way. In other cases, it is clearly consciously cooked, such as Fox News' decision to stop using the term 'suicide bombers' and use 'homicide bombers' instead. However you feel about that, it is obvious that the daily bombardment with a particular term matters and has significant power to shape reality.

We have our own good dose of unspeak in business organizations but let's jump to the next theme of conversation.

Meaning

▶ The 'Sokal Syndrome'

The 1966 Spring/Summer special issue of Social Text - an academic, 'fashionable American cultural studies journal' - featured an article entitled *Transgressing the Boundaries: towards a transformative hermeneutics of quantum gravidity*. It was written by Alan Sokal, a professor of Physics at New York University. It was 'full of absurdities'. It proclaimed the most irrational of propositions and asserted conclusions of the so-called 'post-modernist' type, where everything is relative (from morality to physics) and where science - like everything else - is a social construct.

The whole article was written by linking ridiculous arguments, using unclear or inaccurate terminology and drawing conclusions from totally irrational thought pathways.

But it was happily published! Afterwards, an astonished Sokal went public declaring that it was a hoax! He had shown, through what he called an 'unorthodox and uncontrolled experiment', that one can get away with almost anything in these times of cultural fashion and questionable judgement.

The debate had just started. Front pages of *The New York Times, The International Herald Tribune*, the UK's *Observer* and the French *Le Monde*, all carried the news of the hoax. But what started as a contained provocation, soon extended to a debate on the broader issue of using sophisticated language borrowed from contemporary physics and mathematics and applying it to social sciences – a typical 'post-modernist' debate!

▶ *Intellectual Impostures*

What was next? A book, first in French and then in English. *Intellectual Impostures* (Profile Books, 1999) was written by Sokal with the friendly help of Jean Bricmont, another physics professor, this time from Europe (Louvain, Belgium). The book is a devastating criticism on 'la crème de la crème' of mainly, but not only, French intellectuals and their use of scientific terms that, according to some, they don't understand, to pontificate on psychological/social/linguistic/ political issues.

Having trained in Psychiatry, I particularly enjoyed reading the chapter on the French psychoanalyst Jacques Lacan who, amongst other things, used mathematical terminology to talk about psychological and linguistic topics. As a student, I never understood a word of what Lacan had written. For a long time I considered myself the owner of a second-class brain unable to grasp intellectual constructs of the likes of Lacan. Sokal and Bricmont redeemed me. A bit late, but still.

The authors soon became heroes. Articles proliferated, both for and against them, which were consolidated in a website. A few years later I found myself invited to the launch of Le Laboratoire du Future, and enjoyed dinner with the organizers and delegates in Paris, in the company of prominent names from social sciences, business and politics. Five minutes later on, we were talking about 'the Sokal affair'. A famous sociologist confessed to me that many of 'those French intellectuals' had, for some reason, become heroes within the American academia and intelligentsia. As far as he was concerned, he had never understood what all the fuss was about.

▶ *Jargon pollution and mind graffiters*

Organizational life, business leadership: all have their own 'Sokal syndrome', inundated by jargon and often meaningless terminology. It may not have been borrowed from physics, but it suffers the same Sokalian disease. The only advantage is that sometimes business-guru-jargon is less pretentious and one can spot prêt-a-porter garbage more easily, without having to spend a lot of time debating whether or not the problem is in your genetically limited brain. In other words, the hesitation (*"Am I missing something?"*, *"Am I an idiot?"*) is usually shorter, sometimes of nanosecond magnitude. I want to propose that one of the primary roles of the modern leader should be to uncover 'intellectual nudity'. And we have a lot of that around.

As I have mentioned before, we are also creating a bullet-point society leading to 'The End of Judgement'. In this societal model, arguments must be summarized in three bullet points and judgement must be condensed on the basis of a 'give-me-the-net-net' statement. It is, of course, the sound bite society that the current educational system is creating in most western countries.

Business dynamics and their 'functional pillars' (organizational development, Human Resources, strategy-systems-structure setting, operational practices and so on) need strong cultivation of judgement plus plain English. If what is needed is to shout *"The emperor has no clothes!"*, so be it. Somebody on the payroll may need to stand up and say, *"My dear guru who is influencing our current rhetoric and business practices, you have the intellectual strength of a cream cake. Thanks for your contributions. I am going to exercise what is left of my brain."* It may be just one of these revolutionary behaviours that could make the difference.

▶ What is the question?

Picture this. One sunny morning at Princeton, Albert Einstein's assistant was confronted with an unexpected problem. She had just seen the professor's draft for the final exams that year and could see that it was just like last year's paper. Was he becoming forgetful, or just a bit old? Maybe this was a sign of decline in the great Bavarian refugee who had taught at Zurich, Prague and Berlin and who had ended up teaching mathematical physics in the US. The man who had changed much of the previous understanding of the universe could not see that he was going to ask his students the same mathematical questions as last year! All the answers to previous problems and papers had been widely circulated so the students were going to have a ball! Unless she did something about it.

"Professor, I am sorry, but may I just point out that you have given me this year's exam paper, and the questions are, exactly the same as last year's," she said.

"Yes, I know, the questions are the same, but the answers are different," he replied.

If that was true of mathematics and physics in the 1940s, perhaps our world in general has always been, and will always be, the antithesis of stability and predictability. I always refer to this Einstein anecdote when talking about change and 'old and new models' as it seems as if the same questions – political, socio-economic, technical, psychological – keep coming back and the only thing we can be certain about is that the answers are going to be different.

In modern organizational and business life the questions have not changed much: what's the best way of organising the enterprise, what are the potential strategies, how do you manage productivity. The answers change all the time, in most cases influenced by fashion and/or political correctness, rather than reason.

The single most important management question is *"What's the question?"* If every time we were ready to jump to the next decision, the next initiative, the next action, the leader stood back and said, "W*ait a minute, what's the question we are trying to answer?"*, we all would be better off. Again, the question may be the same, but it's worth articulating it anyway because the answer may be very different!

Usually, creating answers is not our problem. We are masters of providing them, but far poorer generators of good questions. Many leaders are by far good providers of beautiful, sophisticated answers to the wrong questions. And one of the most powerful leadership answers may be *"I don't know."* How powerful, provocative, possibly honest and potentially engaging is it in some cases to say: *"I don't know and, quite frankly, I don't think you know either"*?

That's the issue. Leaders in organizations seem sometimes to have lost the ability to acknowledge that 'they don't know'. People expect answers. Leaders feel that they should provide them and that not doing so, is simple weakness. So, sometimes, anything goes. The 'answer' is made up with whatever is necessary. The gaps of uncertainty are now filled. All looks pristine like a slide pack for a stock analysts meeting. There may be little substance, but, abundance of nonsense is seen as better than void spaces.

In Gandhi[2], the great 1982 film, there is a fantastic sequence when he arrives to India from South Africa. Ben Kingsley plays Gandhi with incredible skill. Gandhi is received by a crowd at the port. Political figures are welcoming him. His reputation as human rights lawyer and freedom fighter in South Africa is well-known. Expectations are high. A big speech is on the cards. He comes down from the ship's steps. Silence. An overwhelmed-looking Gandhi hesitates. Then the

---

[2] Gandhi, 1982, Carolina Bank Ltd & National Film Development Corporation Ltd

freedom-liberation-independence-to-India-kick-the-Brits-out expected speech starts: *"Thank you, thank...you... I am... very glad to be here...."* Stop. End. All stunned. Gandhi didn't fill in the space for the sake of doing so. He perhaps didn't know what to say. He had the courage of keeping the blank space as such. And I personally think it was one of the best speeches! The crowd starts moving and he does the same. He is bombarded with questions of the like: *"So Mr Gandhi, are you going to do so and so, are you planning to go to A and B, what are you going to do with X, say to Y?"* And the human rights-fighter-lawyer-hope-of-the-nation-high-expectation-leader says, *"I don't know."*

Intention

The third dimension of 'what leaders say' has to do with the intention of the leader and the effect on the (potential) followers. Some people still confuse inspiration (and inspirational leadership) with charisma. Not all leaders need to be of the King school. Actually, many well-run organizations have leaders who wouldn't pass the charisma test. Leaders influence not only through the speak. By definition, all Seven Faces are sources of influence because influence is at the core of the definition of leadership! But I am bringing influence here mainly from the angle of 'what the leader says'.

Two things I'd like to propose to you:

- Different styles of leadership use different styles of influence mechanisms.

- More importantly, the leader is not always aware of the ones he or she is using and a reflection on those would be enlightening!

Influencing pathways and their effects are diverse. Here are what I think to be some of the high-level effects produced by 'what leaders say':

- Effect on thought or opinion, maybe a change in direction
- Triggering or mobilizing commitment to action
- Making me/you be part of a shared vision or common purpose ("*I can relate to that*")
- Generating empathy via a language that 'clicks' with you
- Overall 'engagement': I am now part of this, or proud of being part of this.

▶ *Generic influence*

Influence mechanisms have long been studied by social sciences. We all use a mixture of them. We seem to believe that we know the ones we personally use but it is always surprising to see how much we don't know about other mechanisms that we perhaps use but are not aware of.

Here is my list of seven main mechanisms for reflection:

- **Rational appeals:** B is better than A, we must go for B, these are the facts and the reasons. (And perhaps, "*come with me to do B*", the invitational aspect is always possible). We all think this is our main way of articulating things because we all like to think of ourselves as rational people.

- **Inspirational appeals:** This is fantastic, we are saving lives, we have destiny in our hands.

- **Legitimization**: We must do so, the CEO is expecting it, the Holy Father has requested it. It's the authority above us.

- **Personal appeal**: Do it for me, hey, it's me, your pal, your friend who is asking you. Consistently, many of my clients insist they never use it. I smile, they smile, we move on.

- **Reciprocity**: I am appealing to you now that I need you, I will be there for you when you'll need me.

- **Warnings**: If we don't do so, the sky will fall (or we'll bear the consequences, in other words).

- **Reward (promise):** You'll be rewarded, we will be rewarded, now, in the next life etc.

There are other 'tactics' widely used in the worlds of advertising, political marketing or social influence of some sort:

- **Social proof:** This is a powerful mechanism. Everybody is doing this, a-million-monkeys-can't-be-wrong, A, B and C have already got it, this is what has worked in Z.

- **Scarcity**: We must hurry up, not much left, this is our last chance. Mastered by TV home-shopping channels: buy now, it is on sale. And a little black box on screen saying 'only 7 left'.

- **Ingratiation**: You are good people, intelligent, reasonable. I am proud of being part of this team. Let's do so and so.

- **Consultation**: We are in this together, it is our collective choice, I don't decide, we decide.

- **Coalitions**: We are in this together *with* powerful X and Y, with the fighters of freedom, with the great people of Z.

I am raising these things here to make the point that we are sometimes not aware of our intentional mechanisms. It is part of our emotional intelligence (or lack thereof) that we will discuss briefly in another chapter. Confronted with this list of influencing mechanisms, people sometimes react with dislike; as if these mechanisms all sound like forms of manipulation. If we were to digress into this conversation regarding the ethics of it, we will be jumping to... another book. I'd like to suggest for this conversation that it is just healthy in itself to make the effort of being aware of the mechanisms that we are using. And, believe me, the idea that we are all rational people using rational appeals, is nonsense.

▶ *Horizons*

Gary Hamel and C K Prahalad in their great book *Competing for the future* (Harvard Business School Press, 1994) defined three attributes of Strategic Intent for organizations. I deeply believe that they are three good dimensions of leadership as well and therefore three 'intentions' in the creation of influence. I use them all the time.

- **A sense of direction**. What leaders say is often the most visible vehicle for creating a direction, a sense of future, of possibilities and pathways. Perhaps Livingstone's quote is remarkably relevant here:

  The history of mankind might be described by a cynic as a series of splendid expeditions towards the wrong goal or towards no goal at all, led by men who have all the gifts of leadership except a sense of direction, and every endowment for achieving their ends except a knowledge of ends worth achieving.[3]

- **A sense of discovery**. Leader's language should perhaps point towards exploring new angles, new things or territories. Perhaps leadership directions could be defined as intentionally avoiding the trap of 'managing the inevitable' and switching to leading what could not happen without us! We spend most of the nine-to-five life in organizations managing the inevitable, managing what perhaps would happen anyway!

---

[3] Livingstone, Sir Richard, 1988, *Education for a World adrift*, Tabb House

- **A sense of destiny.** When I use this trio in my leadership seminars and programmes I can always spot the cynical mind somewhere in the room. I am not (or not necessarily) talking about big- capital-Destiny a la Gandhi. There is great small-d destiny around us, which depends on us and only us: we are the ones who will take the organization from A to B, who will put X on the market, who will solve Y forever, who will set up Z. This sense of our unique role, small-d destiny is very powerful!

▶ Speak, meaning and intention

The language of leadership is our first port of call. That's why I have started the Seven Faces promenade here. It is what we hear - from leaders in the corporate environment, in the public services office; in the political leaders' announcements - that very often represents the trigger for everything else.

The message behind the concept of the Seven Faces is that leadership goes well beyond the rhetoric! But we can't ignore the power of the word. Any leader, leader-to-be, reflective reader, you, me, should stop and think a bit about this 'what we say'.

Saying is sometimes the beginning of believing! There is something powerful about the expression:

> *I told them once and they didn't understand*
> *I told them twice and they didn't understand,*
> *I told them three times and I understood!*

Questions

Speak, meaning and intention are the three components of the 'what you say' face. Let's recap and reflect upon them via 'questions'. This is my suggested list, but it will never be complete until you add your own questions.

- Use the list to trigger new questions or to attempt to answer them! Make notes, use the book!
- Commit to one single step to 'answer the question'. These steps may look like actions you want to take, questions you want to ask other people in your organization or 'practice' that you want to do at your next opportunity.

Speak

- Do I know about my language?
- Am I bullet-pointing everybody around me?
- Do I tend to use a metrics-only language? The milestones we need to hit, the market-share we need to gain or the cost-cuttings we need to achieve?
- Do I appeal, any dent-in-the-universe? Could I do it?
- Am I invitational? Do I use "*join me*", "*come with me*", "*let's do it together*"?
- Is there any 'dream' in my language? Goals? Both? Have I distinguished between these in the past?
- Is my language an 'I' language or a 'we' language?
- Do I use bipolar rhetoric? Am I a black-and-white leader from speak point-of-view?
- How much 'tyranny of the or' do I use?

- Is my leadership language full of jargon or perhaps 'unspeak'?
- Does my speak usually provide more questions than answers? Does it matter? Should I reflect upon that balance?
- Do I always have an answer? Is this expected from me?

Meaning

- Does my speak have any Sokal-like features? Does my speak 'substance' make sense?
- Am I using borrowed language from somewhere else and apply it to my speak to appear better informed or more 'clever'?
- Am I perhaps a 'mind polluter', a 'mind graffiter'?
- Am I clear and meaningful? Do I know?
- How much of 'bottom lines', 'net-nets', 'game-plans', 'empowerment' and other business jargon am I using?
- Do I provide meaning with those? Am I doing OK, or overdoing it?
- Am I using the *"What's the question?"* question enough?
- Could I say/do I say *"I don't know"*? What are the implications?

Intention

- Am I aware of the influence of my speak?
- Do I create empathy, or engagement, or curiosity, or..?
- What's usually the reaction?
- Do I sense that I mobilize commitment or create engagement with my speak?

- What are my routine 'influence mechanisms'? Rational appeals? Inspirational? Appeals to higher authority? Personal calls and appeals? Appeals to reciprocity? Promises of rewards? Warnings of punishments or negative consequences?
- Do I feel I trigger 'Direction'? 'Destiny'? 'Discovery'?

ACTION MAP
(some first pass questions)

Me   **My organization**

Me

Questions:
Am I aware of my 'language', of the style and influence of my speak?

Questions:
What messages am I giving? Am I properly translating a vision or a shared world? Am I providing meaning?

My organization

Questions:
How does the organization 'hear' me? What would I hear if I were in their shoes?

Questions:
What's our organizational language? What kind of world are we creating with it? How does our language influence what we do?

This is a very simple set of questions to get you started
with your reflections and actions. Use the blank pages to
record your own questions and notes

▶ *Your Questions and Notes:*

What you say

▶ *Your Questions and Notes:*

The Leader with Seven Faces

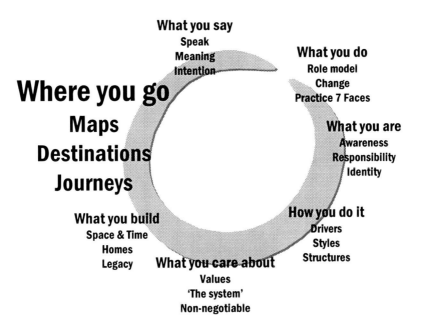

The Leader with Seven Faces

2

Where you go
Maps
Destinations
Journeys

Walker, there is no road. The road is made as you walk.
Antonio Machado[4]

Leaders go places. What a disclosure! So much has been talked about vision, about leaders having an almost exact idea of where to go and taking people with them, that one hardly needs an introduction to the topic. However, for this conversation with you I'd like to propose three dimensions of this 'going places' or, indeed, this 'knowing where to go'.

- **Maps.** In this face of leadership, leaders are cartographers, map-makers. I think that providing 'maps' is an almost inherent characteristic of expressing things, trying to influence and leading. We love maps. Even the ones who say they don't need them, have one in their mind! This book is a kind of map because it offers you some possible highways and country lanes for exercising leadership!

---

[4] Machado, Antonio (1875 – 1939), Walker, there is no road. (Caminante, no hay camino)

- **Destinations.** In this face of leadership, destinations matter. These leaders talk the language of getting somewhere; arriving at a particular time; achieving A, B, C; realizing a vision that takes the organization to a particular place, including a place in history.

- **Journeys.** You can have good maps and good ideas of destinations but if you don't travel the road, you won't get anywhere and will spend your life admiring the maps and admiring the destinations

Maps

▶ *Managing irrationality*

This is for real. Every time the hunting group is ready to go, the same ritual occurs in a particular Indian tribe. One of the elders gathers the men and burns small pieces of wood in a ceremonious way. The shape of the ashes after a few mixes and movements in the flat container has shown the elder the direction for the hunters: north, south, east, up the mountain, down the valley, etc. People dance, hunters get ready, elder indicates the way to go according to the ashes. This is a community where hunting is a key part of their way of life. They are not only good at the use of hunting tools but also very successful in their escapades. Coming back with 'food' is the norm. The key behind their success is in those ashes. The ashes determine where to go. Not terribly scientific for our standards, but this is not the point. How the whole thing works, is!

There is an unwritten principal behind this irrationality leading to success. The logical and rational thing to do for a hunting party is to go back to the place where they found the animals last time. If animals abound east of the camp and down in the forest, why on earth would anybody want to go west and up the hills?

If you were a management consultant to these Indians, you would surely recommend to them that they repeat a successful process and develop expertise! Maybe - dare I say? - you would tell them that they should create a core competence around that standard process! Aside from the catatonic face of Chief Asher when you talk to him in these terms, your advice would be wrong.

You would be advising rationality when irrationality is what feeds them. If the hunting party goes to the same place every time and is successful every time, the result is that the area will be progressively depleted of animals. The ashes introduce a random strategy that - by forcing the hunters to go in several directions without much repetition – is bound to make them find animals without depleting the areas. The irrational ashes have a rational logic after all.

Scenario two. The battalion is in full survival exercise in the middle of the Alps. As such, their conditions are deliberately harsh and the whole idea is to test ways to survive with little or no support. Everything goes well until the weather suddenly changes and heavy snow and storms flood the place. The drill is no drill anymore. It's pure reality testing. They didn't anticipate this.

The situation of the group becomes progressively dangerous. Some people reach freezing thresholds. Something serious must be done, but their decision capacity on what to do has become a bit paralysed. Activity is better than the alternative so they know that they must walk. The question is, in which direction?

Suddenly, one of the soldiers pulls out a map which was hidden in his kit. He was probably not supposed to have it but, quite frankly, they are not in the business of debating discipline now! The map is more than welcome. It takes them a few seconds to figure out a route that they must follow to go back to base. The map clearly shows them the straight path along the valley, over that hill, and reaching the base across the river. And they move. A few hours later, exhausted but alive, they reach the base. It was great to have a map whether they were supposed to have it or not! They celebrate over hot drinks. Once settled, they have a chance to look at the map again, but now with some calm. It was a map of the Pyrenees. They had just survived in the Alps!

▶ *Any map welcome*

Both vignettes/stories are true. In both cases, action was induced and inaction prevented. In both cases, the outcome is successful adaptation. The Indians went in the direction of the ashes and statistically increased their chance of finding animals. The soldiers in the Alps were saved by the existence of a (wrong) map that made them move.

The Indians behaviour and method – 'irrational' to us, 'rational' to them - save them. The soldiers' rational (to us and them) behaviour, based upon a rational (to us and them) method, saves them, even if all is based upon completely wrong information.

Daily life in organizations provides us with continuous examples of these combinations: wrong assumptions but good success, right information but total failure, irrational thinking that delivers the goods, rational behaviour that destroys something, etc. We have a tremendous ability to use post hoc fallacies. That is: B follows A, so A causes B. Good planning is followed by project success, so it must be because of the planning. Good training increases sales; so, there you are, sales are the consequence of the effort. New leader comes in and company has turnaround; good news, turnaround is due to the leader we have just hired.

▶ Fooled by randomness

Post hoc fallacies are an incredibly good anti-anxiety drug for the brain, better than taking tranquilizers. They tell us that our actions make sense and that the world around us is rational, ergo, manageable by us, rational people. We like the connections between A and B. We love causality. We may be 'fooled by randomness'[5] but, hey, who cares, the causal story linking A and B is always a good one.

A closer look at the reality could perhaps tell us a different story. Not necessarily, but possibly. For example, that the project success was due not to the extraordinary planning but

---

[5] Taleb, Nassim Nicholas, 2004, *Fooled by Randomness: The Hidden Role of Chance in Life and in The Markets*, Thomson Texere, New York

to some heroic actions of some people. That the increased sales were not due to the outstanding training of the sales force but to the pathetic performance of a key competitor. That the turnaround of the company had nothing to do with the new leader but with the measures put in place by the old one who was fired before he could see the benefits of them. And so on...

Despite our affinity to believe that the world around us is rational, we are a production machine of irrational behaviours. We may find the Indians esoteric, but we may be seen as such ourselves by other observers. We have this need to declare rationality as the norm, because otherwise there would be no parameters to judge or logic to follow.

The whole discipline of economics is based upon the assumption of rationality. Given the option - i.e. given knowledge of alternatives and outcomes - people will opt for a rational behaviour that maximizes the utility. This is the foundation of all economics. In plain English, we expect people to behave rationally and mainly in their own interests, whether it's personal or a group interest.

The whole economics architecture is, of course, flawed because the assumption is no longer sustainable. The 'branch' of Behavioural Economics studies these irrational inconsistencies of people or markets, which can't be understood under the principle, mother of the discipline.

So, are we all Indians playing with ashes and deciding where to go, or soldiers making it despite wrong maps? Is it unpredictable chaos around us despite our determination to see logic and order?

The Chief Asher Manager and the soldier who shouts, *"Give me that damned map, let's get out of here and forget the drill!"* were the leaders. But both act upon a wrong set of assumptions, one intrinsically irrational, the other false but effective! Are all leaders like them?

▶ Assumption traps

What strikes me is how much of our organizational life (processes, decisions, 'logic') is based upon assumptions of rationality when, just outside the window, we would see a rather different world. Let me give you an example. A data provider company serves a customer by delivering huge amounts of market information. That information, it's assumed, will be the basis for good resource allocation decisions, which in turn, it's assumed, will lead to success.

This formula has worked for donkey's years. But the whole logic algorithm is often flawed. The existence of available and ready-to-use information is unfortunately no guarantee for good decision making. Managers make good decisions with lousy information and bad decisions with excellent data.

The logic also assumes that people who receive the information will actually use it, which is a hell of an assumption. Very often the assumed route of the information flow is totally theoretical, as a good knowledge flow mapping exercise would perhaps show.

Finally, it also assumes that managers, in general, will act rationally in the assessment of the information, that they will make the consequent and consistent resource allocation decisions, and that those in turn will lead to that market share increase. Again, an incredible amount of wishful thinking on this journey, but we want to believe that this is how it works

► Challenging rationality

Managing irrationality and leading through it, is a forgotten core leadership competence, to use the jargon. It's not about throwing in the towel and declaring that 'it's madness out there' and that therefore anything is possible. But it's about:

- being aware that we are very irrational animals, equipped with a fairly rational thinking tool inside the skull.
- the leader having to challenge the apparent lines of rationality, scratching the surface and trying to find those assumptions, the consistency of which may be as strong as jelly.
- not dismissing the role of irrationality itself - what I call the remember-the-hunters warning - because it may contain some good adaptive solutions that rationality itself may lack.
- Above all, it is about not mistaking irrationality with emotionality. Many people believe that the opposite of rational is emotional. And in business terms 'emotional' almost always has a negative connotation. If we say a leader is not a good one because he acts very emotionally sometimes, we are saying that we expect rationality and detachment. 'Emotionally' here, literally means 'not good for business'. But the true opposite to rationality is irrationality, whilst the true opposite to emotional is unemotional. You can be

rational and emotional (our brain is this all the time) and also irrational and emotional etc.

In general, business management hasn't even got the equivalent of behavioural economics. The Society for the Advance of Behavioural Economics (SABE) states that it *"welcomes the use of psychology, sociology, history, political science, biology, and other disciplines to assist in furthering our understanding of economic choice."* No such thing in business management. I would be happy with just a tenth of it! We all, apparently, make rational decisions based on rational data. That is, we hunt in the same area where we hunted before and that gives us that 3.4 % increase in market share, with the same repeated process. And it's all ISO9000. It pleases the City and Wall Street. Do modern leaders need some pieces of wood and a box of matches?

▶ *In God we trust, others bring maps*

Airports in summer are Darwinian landscapes where your survival instincts take over from other more civilized inclinations, such as being polite to your neighbours or restraining yourself from hitting them with an overweight rucksack. In the part of the world where I live - England - we have reinvented low-fare airlines as a carbon copy of the American Southwest's. These airlines are often called 'no frills', but should be re-branded as 'no-manners'. As a heavy user of one particular airline - their employees are banned from charging their mobile phones in company buildings (it's considered as stealing corporate electricity!) and have to pay for their own uniforms and soft drinks on the plane - I know what I am talking about!

In some airports the toxicity of the no-frills-no-manners ethos seems to have gone beyond the airline desk. The rest of the airport paraphernalia, such as increased security, doesn't help either. On a bad day, the airport experience is one of sadomasochistic proportions. On a good day, you might just find a polite employee who smiles.

The airport bookshops are good retreats from these jungles and I spend quite a bit in them, mostly browsing and finding out what is on the shelves. There are two types of books hugely over-represented, no matter which airport you're at. One is the conspiracy-thriller-pseudo-history with - at the time of writing - Dan Brown's collection of Da Vinci Code, demons, angels and the rest at the front, along with another dozen or so authors with books covering the spectrum of religion, politics and global domination by world powers.

The other type is the 'self-help-how-to' one, which in most cases shares shelf space with psychology! With my behavioural sciences and medical background, I can't resist looking at those shelves where often the only real psychology is the label on the bookshelf, not its tenants.

Self–help is a huge industry now close to 10 billion US dollars a year. Its gurus write for and advise a full spectrum of society and they consult with CEOs, heads of state, community leaders and airport nomads.

The borders with religion, humanistic values, health, business, New Age, social issues, etc. are often hard to find, but it would be too easy to dismiss the whole thing as a charlatan-like epidemic of colossal proportions.

I have done a quick and dirty research into what I call 'the universal scripts'. Here they are, as far as I am concerned:

1 The 'learn from me' model: I did it, you can do it as well, here's how.
2 How to change (your life,?) in 30 days and other step-by-step plans.
3 The world before you is unlimited, don't constrain yourself to a limited path.
4 Here are some types of (people, situations…). Find the fit and follow the instructions.
5 Here is the (experiential) evidence: somebody (some company?) found himself in this and did that.
6 Here is a method/trick/way, repeat again and again, it works.
7 You are at the centre, you are in charge, reward yourself, you are great.
8 Don't judge, see all the angles, all is relative, understand and comprehend, then you'll see differently.
9 Just do it, stop whinging and procrastinating, move!
10 Pick and mix, take what suits you, what you like. You can leave the rest, you don't have to agree with everything.
11 Rely on a 'higher power' (religious, spiritual?), let it go.
12 Trust your intuition, your feelings (or don't look for rationality).

There you have it, twelve pristine plots, twelve scripts, twelve maps (which in itself is an example of number four!), and all can be reduced to categories… These themes cut across a broad spectrum: from individual self-help and motivation to business management; from collective intellectual wisdom to practical 'this is what you need to do'; from spiritual and religious connotations to prosaic streetwise realities. It's all mixed together on the same airport bookshelves. Divinity and Zen meet Covey, meet biography, meet cookbook methodology, meet Jack Welch, meet DYI, meet self-esteem injection. I have a better idea for the label in the bookshop. Forget self-help or 'psychology' or 'lifestyle' or even 'business'. Write 'maps! All these are maps; the big industry is Cartography.

Through my behavioural sciences glasses, my own reductionism of all these scripts is even simpler:

1. You have lots of possibilities, you are rich but you may not know it.
2. Choose.
3. Stop analyzing, just do it.
4. I've done it, you can do it too.

You can construct a whole sub-industry of self-help themes around plots containing combinations of the four above. But that's a story for another day.

▶ Naked leadership

I met David Taylor at a dinner recently. You may not know who David is, but there is a statistical chance you have had one of his books in your hands if you are the type of airport nomad that I am. He is the author of, among other titles, *The naked leader*[6]. The book is a compilation of wisdom, formula,

---

[6] Taylor, David, 2002, *The Naked Leader*, Capstone Publishing, Oxford (UK)

motivation and other ideas, none of them original. I can't think of anything in the book that has not been written elsewhere. It almost contains my twelve universal scripts. There is nothing new in there. The overriding proposed formula - know where you want to go, assess the gap, move in that direction (this is my paraphrasing) - is hardly breakthrough thinking.

The book and its follow-up are full of examples, quotes, suggestions, provocations and attempt to build your own self-esteem ('what if you could not fail'). It is light, very light, very simple. You would have thought maybe even irrelevant. The book has been translated into 38 languages and it is a fantastic success. David travels the world giving speeches, talking to CEOs, providing wisdom and making a living from the lot. David is, by any account, an extremely successful writer-guru in the motivation-inspiration-self-help-leadership arena. *The Naked Leader* is a great success book that contains no new thinking, no new theory, no new inspiration, no discovery of a new method, no new research, no new model of leadership.

There are two reasons for David's success. One I knew after reading the books and well before my accidental meeting with David Taylor at the dinner party. The other I learnt only after meeting him in person. The first one has to do with David being a cartographer. He sells maps. The book is a map, or better, a collection of many maps. As a map maker, David himself has not created the geography; he just draws the connections and paints the landscape.

Here is the secret: people need maps. I said it at the beginning. This is a rather stupid statement but it is the best I can think of to explain how we are all desperate for the maps that tell us how to go from A to B, what the options are, how to get there faster or slower, where to stop. A map tells us that there are some possibilities, that the journey is possible. It also gives you some reassurances that you'll get there. There are geographical maps, spiritual journey maps, personal development maps, strategy maps, business plan maps, children's education maps, political maps, relationship maps. These maps are usually available to us via our teachers, mentors, parents, political leaders, bosses, religious figures, writers, gurus and airport business school authors. The quality of the maps varies but their availability and quantity is huge.

A good business leader, we often say, tells us about the strategy and the journey to get there and provides a set of objectives and rules. A religious leader may appeal to higher powers and translate the journey for the flock. A political leader does the same. It's all cartography. As I said at the beginning of this chapter, even the ones who reject maps, who don't want to follow instructions or dictations, or who want to create their own pathways, have a map. They may not know it, but it will be somewhere in their mind.

The second reason for David's success is David himself, but I needed an unexpected dinner invitation to know that. David Taylor is not only a good cartographer of pathways, writer of books with no new ideas, no new research, no original breakthrough thinking, but he is also a good, honest human being. The statements about the lack of originality that I have made so far would not trouble him. On the contrary, his key point would be that 'it's all out there in life', all written in previous business books (which he has researched extensively) and that the secret is that there is no secret. David

Taylor genuinely wants to change the world and believes in the ability of people to boost their self-esteem and 'do it'. He himself is involved in a significant number of charity/non-profit initiatives. David is an honest cartographer who says, *"I haven't invented the geography; I have put together some maps."* David is a good teacher-leader-cartographer.

There is an abundance of map makers. They sit in Parliament or Congress, they preach in worship places, they teach in schools (including business schools), they are invited to express their views and show their maps on primetime TV, they write books, they produce tapes and videos, they give after-dinner speeches and charge for motivational-inspirational retreats. Some of them are enlightening, liberating and enhancers of your own self-esteem, others are pretty dangerous.

▶ *Too many maps*

Maps are also not in short supply within the corporation. They take the form of strategic frameworks, credos, quality lists, mission and vision statements, change principles, leadership principles, sales principles, performance management systems, scorecards, scoreboards, etc. The reason why organizations produce that myriad of frameworks is because there always seems to be a need to produce yet another map, another set of guidelines and another set of criteria. The problem is that people often get bombarded with one map after another.

Big organizations suffer from initiative fatigue often triggered by the interests of internal functional groups, all of them with the best of intentions trying to produce references for people. In my work with sales organizations, I have often encountered situations described to me as 'a world of initiatives running in never convergent ways'. A sales director counted them for me:

- A Performance Management System for all sales people.
- A Sales Leadership Process (SLP) establishing methods and steps for everybody to follow.
- A 'Quality of Leadership' campaign.
- An Incentive scheme, in itself described as a combination of different targets.
- A corporate driven 'Customer First' credo translated into five sets of 'attitudes'.
- A Management 'Balance Scorecard'.

These six systems/processes/initiatives/measurements/sets-of-maps were running in parallel at a given time. For people in the field force it was impossible to even remember some of them, let alone to see any kind of connections. The 'system' was so complex that many employees had literally given up the hope of making any sense of it and were content with doing their jobs as well as they could.

There have been some cynical scenes where people have told management - often in the comfortable environment of a social evening after a business workshop - *"whatever you want! I just can't track anything anymore!"*

Maps are extremely useful. Map fatigue is a serious problem. Leaders-cartographers must create maps that make sense and that people can follow.

▶ Beyond the maps

I'd like to suggest that at reflection time, pretty much at the end of the chapter, you ask yourself how much of a cartographer you are. But for now, let's continue this conversation beyond maps, and talk about destinations and journeys. Allow me to point out that not only do I personally have no problem with cartography in itself being a form of leadership (!) but that I believe that many times we are better off having only the map and not having a clear destination or an idea of the journey. *"Anathema!"* many will shout, *"Is leadership not about knowing where to go, and expressing it, and taking people along with you?"* I can quote many super-academics saying this. Usually these are also the ones that believe that leadership needs the solid three: knowing exactly where to go, plus having exactly the right map, plus travelling the exact journey (and taking people with you).

I feel sorry for this concept of leadership. It puts vision at the top of the tops. Vision must be strong, well-defined, clear. Destination is fixed. There we go!

Destinations

Fixed ideas terrify me. Fixed ideas are not the same as strong ideas. Fixed means no discussion, usually because I am in the total possession of the truth, either via some sort of genetic predisposition to exactness or divine inspiration. If vision is indisputable, an unmovable idea of where to go, men of vision scare me. I suggest you should at least be a bit scared as well.

In the quest for arrival at the vision-point, visionary leaders of the type trust-me-I-am-the-one-with-the-vision-everybody-else-needs-glasses are very dangerous.

Whoever thinks that in today's world we have fixed, unmovable points of destination, needs a bit of reality checking. Many organizations have gone down because of too much visionary leadership. Visionary leadership's rigidity doesn't leave room for alternatives, for change of direction, for mobility and fast adaptation. It is, or it becomes, destination-at-any-cost. The more fixed ideas about destiny there are, the weaker the organization. The opposite of that is not necessarily to propose totally flexible, non-directional, non-fixed-destination leadership.

► Destination leadership

Destination-leadership needs a bit of historical thinking and reference. Spanish conquistadores left the Castilian and Estremadura planes in search of new worlds. And, as we know, not with good maps! Christopher Columbus had to keep on trying (four times!) before hitting the American mainland and other conquistadores were well aware that they were heading for terra incognita. The leader-conquistador had ideas of destiny but had enough built-in flexibility to change directions, targets or pace. He had no choice!

I know, I know, that saying, again: "*If you don't know where you are going, any road will take you there.*" I know that it is risky to stand up in front of your organization and say, "*let's go, not sure where to, but let's go!*" You'll be told that your doubts disqualify you as a leader, that the journey will be dangerous without knowledge about the journey. You'll perhaps say that it is somewhere in north-west direction, but that you're not sure exactly and what's the problem with that? And you'll be told to come back when you are a good leader, when you know where exactly in the North-West it is that you mean. But what's wrong with moving, exploring, leaving the Castilian planes for terra incognita?

▶ The art of moving

Robert Kane, professor of Philosophy at the University of Texas in Austin, tells the story of an MBA student who went back to his old campus for his 10-year reunion. He had a brief encounter with the dean in the cafeteria.

"Dean, remember graduation day? You were on stage trying to drive the long procession of students at a pace to get our diplomas. We were both slow and overwhelmed. From the corner of the stage you kept telling us in your deep voice: Keep moving! Keep moving! You know, Dean? That was the best business advice given to me on all those three years. This is what I have been doing since!"

That little story may tell a thing or two about the lasting effects of business education. MBAs curricula share with Chinese meals the perception of abundance and the lack of fullness. Apparently, the student could not clearly remember the academic portfolio of strategic choices or economic value added, but the 'keep moving' of his last day struck a chord in his brain.

There is more to the 'keep moving' story than the anecdote may tell. Perhaps 'keep moving' is the real quintessence of organizational life: moving in a direction, any direction, but moving above all. Is there a list of 'the most admired companies that *just move*'?

I can hear the strategists and planners saying that this is nonsense, that one has to know where one is going, otherwise…Have you heard it before? Any road would get you nowhere. Fine, but let's be aware of the other end of the spectrum. The one where the 'Ultimate Unmoveable Goal' sits. Let's have a vision, a very concrete goal and let's move forward in that direction (at more or less steam depending on the competition), no questions asked, all of us aligned, one, two, three, here we go! As the story says, some people spend all their life climbing up a ladder against the wrong wall. The same happens with companies and organizations with destination-only leadership.

Perhaps the mixture of humility to identify the wrong wall – even if half climbed already – and drive to move somewhere else, is what strategy is about. Canadian Professor Henry Mintzberg's metaphor of strategy is not the conventional linear one: a goal in the future and a straight line to get there. Strategy to him is closer to clay modelling than to target shooting. You make it up as you go along. The problem is that a journey with different pathways, change of directions, temporarily getting lost in the forest, coming out back to dry road, keep moving, resting and starting again, may not meet the expectations of The City or Wall Street. Sustained, consistent, predictable, unsurprising, linear, successful, quarter after quarter increased earnings results is what counts. No room for meandering here. When the business model is the Ultimate Goal of Continuous Success Walking the Predefined Trail of Strategy, there is only one pathway: a straight motorway or highway, probably with loads of tolls to pay.

► *In rehearsal mode*

From a leadership behavioural perspective the 'keep moving metaphor' is far from trivial. As I said before, conventional business wisdom tends to support the idea that there is no point in moving until you know in which direction and/or to where. Fine. That's why we do so much situation analysis, so much salami slicing of reality, so much market research, so much strategic analysis, so much strategic planning on pretty much anything as long as the word 'strategic' is in front. Perhaps because of my unapologetic bias towards behavioural sciences, I profess this deep philosophical belief, often translated into this trivial prescription: when in doubt, move!

Moving, moving, moving, gives you more chances of finding the pathway and of defining your strategy in the process (yes, in that order) than sitting still and admiring the problem will. 'Moving', whether at personal, professional or organizational level, exposes you to different inputs, different environments and different information channels. It will force your biology/psychology to adapt and react and, in the process - even if some pain is involved - you have a better chance of gaining a better level of … comfort, stability, understanding, growth, or anything else, whether you were looking for it consciously or unconsciously.

Clinical psychology and psychiatry, and also Medicine in general, are full of practical examples where the only apparent solution to a problem is the radical 'shock' to the system (sorry, that's you and me!) often via a 'transplant' to a new environment, and the more alien the better.

Our adaptive capacity is enormous. Sometimes it is only that new environment, even if hostile, that has the power to trigger healing mechanisms unknown to ourselves. It is amazing what people can mobilize in terms of resources in situations such as emigration or sudden change of 'home' (for example, children going to live with relatives following a parent's death).

Why is al this relevant to leadership? Leaders need to avoid the permanent state of rehearsal mode that some organizations and groups live in. We always need more data, more money, more analysis. We reserve the 'real mode' for when we have more power, become promoted, when we will have more headcount. Leaders, I suggest, force the move forward.

The dean's 'keep moving' wasn't trivial. Armed with maps (and as we have seen, even a wrong one may do it!) with some idea of destination (exploratory/discovery mode or pretty clear picture of 'where') and taking people on a journey, leaders sometimes need to declare enough-of-analysis and start the movement. Trial and error is better than paralysis. Prototyping is better than a permanent quest for the perfect time, perfect product, perfect idea and perfect organization.

▶ *Looking for my keys*

A man is searching the grounds of a large garden. He looks behind trees and under bushes in different places, all in one corner of the garden. Another man approaches.

"*What are you doing?*" he asks.

"*I'm looking for my keys, I've lost them,*" says the first man, while continuing to search the undergrowth.

"*Do you know where you lost them?*"

"*Yes, over there,*" says the man, pointing in the opposite direction of where he is searching.

"*Wait a minute,*" says the other man, "*if you lost your keys over there, why are you looking for them over here?*"

"*Because here there is more light.*"

There is nothing like good light to help find lost keys, or answers to questions, or solutions to problems. But often the attraction of a good light makes us forget that the questions and problems may have little to do with the lit territories where we look for answers and solutions. Still, we prefer places where there is more light. We may tend to choose destinations depending on the amount of light available there.

Destination-leadership has to be careful about that. The most luminous points of arrival may not be relevant. The keys may have been lost in the dark areas and you may need a torch or two. Daily leadership is full of examples of 'looking-for-my keys-syndrome'. If we can see it, grab it, count it, modify or do something about it, it seems a good reason to focus the attention on it. But if the problem is obscure, the issue complex, and the topic or the facts 'fuzzy' or 'soft', we often look for solutions in the corner of the garden where there is more light. The answers may be complex and the dealing with the soft and fuzzy issues may not be something we are equipped for. It may be harder in the shade or in the dark, but these may be the places that need our focus.

So, here are a couple of apparently unrelated day-to-day management examples that share the same traits.

The need to 'find money' to balance the yearly budget and deliver targets promised to investors - particularly in the second half of the year - often initiates a familiar ritual: the cutting of the training budget, the travel budget, conference attendances and a 'headcount freeze'. Accountants will give you a number of good and legitimate reasons for these cuts. After all, these are costs one can 'control' (by deciding not to spend).

Firing people in September for budget reasons and then topping up the headcount in January using the new budget has yet to become part of the ritual, to my knowledge. In countries where the severance package is minimal it could be done, I suppose, but I have not come across this Accounting Fundamentalism…yet! And in countries where the severance pay is close to a nice golden parachute, the practice would defeat the objective. In both, the exercise would be a bit stupid but I wouldn't be surprised to discover that it's practiced somewhere. It would not surprise me if Accounting Fundamentalism did search for its lost keys in the well-lit part of the budget garden, that is, those targets that can be counted, costed and supposedly controlled. 'Travel', 'Training' 'Consultants' and 'Conferences', for example, are part of the cost-cutting ritual, sharing the common basket of disposable activities. All these 'things' - whilst outwardly acknowledged as important for the overall development of the company's

I.Q. - are seen by the Financial Guard as suspiciously semi-luxurious or prone-to-waste items. After all, who can put a value (monetary, of course) on training and development, or attendance at a conference or the face-to-face meetings between widespread project teams?

► *Pavlovian Management*

One problem with this Pavlovian management where, when presented with budget shortfalls, the company triggers the kind of 'cuts and freezes' described above, is that it often generates 'preventive strike management behaviour': spend as much as you can on conferences, travel, training and recruitment at the beginning of the year, just in case. But this is not the point. The point is that in many cases those budget lines are simply the ones with more light, the ones where it doesn't take much effort to find savings.

The consequences of such cuts are often neglected. There is no arithmetic in place to assess the cost-of-not-doing: of not having that face-to-face meeting, of delaying that recruitment activity. There may well be other areas where managers could look for savings but often this just isn't on offer. 'Management', or 'Finance', or both, dictate that particular items should be cut, period. They do not give managers the opportunity of finding savings in the shaded areas, as well as the lit part of the garden. Instead, management or finance says: "*We've lost the keys, and you must search over there in those bushes, yes, over there, that sunny area, sorry.*"

I have enough friends in the financial community whose disapproving faces I can picture on hearing those arguments which they will probably consider 'simplistic'. I have also spent enough years dealing with budgets to challenge my 'number friends' to tell me that this life vignette is wrong. Am I suggesting a sort of financial nirvana where there are never cuts? Of course not. If one has to 'find the money', responsible managers will have to do it, period. But they should be allowed to examine the entire garden!

I bring this here as an example of looking for the keys in the luminous part. Leaders who play this game profess the principle that destination is wherever there is more light. You will never find them exploring uncomfortable darkness. The destination is clear. Because there is more light.

A second example is the one of fixing technological issues when the original problem is largely human. At a knowledge management conference I attended a while ago, a brave manager from one of the top pharmaceutical companies was supposed to present on how the whole area of knowledge management had been tackled in her organization. This company is well-known for having so-called knowledge management systems which, seen from the outside, look like a fairly sophisticated IT system to capture, store, share and utilize knowledge in many forms.
The reason I have called her brave is because she told us upfront that she, as senior manager in charge of the programme, recognized that knowledge management programmes and systems are 80% about human capital - about how people learn from each other and share information, their attitudes, mutual trust etc. Only 20 %, she said, was about technology, sophisticated IT systems such as corporate portals. "*We don't know,*" she said, "*how to tackle the 80%, so I will tell you what we have done with the other*

20." The other 20% seemed to have got a few million dollars' investment on unified global IT systems that allowed scientists to find and share information, search for data and look for answers to problems. They certainly had the state-of-the-art technocratic solution.

This honest manager was in charge of producing beautiful technocratic solutions to the wrong problems. And I admired her courage to stand up in front of 300 people and say that she hadn't a clue on how to address the human factors in that business of 'knowledge management'. The IT systems lit up part of the garden and, like the man in the garden, she was honest enough to say the keys were lost somewhere else, but, hey, let's enjoy the sunshine, let me share with you a few hundred PowerPoint slides on how to spend a few million on 20% of the problem.

As different as they are, both the 'Pavlovian Management' and the 'Beautiful solution, wrong problem' case, show there is a sort of leadership magnet drawing us to the easy targets, the things we can control, the visible part of problems. We have an affinity with the tips of icebergs. We sometimes use the term 'focus on the obvious', for example, in order to assist our behaviour. And this is interesting because 'obvious', etymologically, means 'lying in the way', 'meet in the way'. So, the obvious is strictly speaking something that may 'get in the way' and prevent, possibly distort or make us stumble! The obvious, etymologically from Latin, means an obstacle!

Journeys

The journey matters to some leaders. It is not the map, it is not the destination: it's the journey. Needless to say, it may come to you with some oriental smell and spicy flavours because it is very - what we call in the West - Eastern! 'The way' is a Buddhist concept and the journey - a deeply spiritual concept - is incidentally not only Eastern! I like to use this little tale in my leadership seminars:

A young boy travelled across Japan to study with a famous martial artist. The master asked him what he wanted. The young boy told him he wanted to be the finest martial artist in the land and asked how long he had to study. "Ten years at least", the master answered. "But what if I studied twice as hard as all your other students?" the young boy responded. "Twenty years", the master replied. "Twenty years! What if I practice day and night with all my effort?" "Thirty years", was the master's reply. The boy was thoroughly confused. "How is it that each time I say I will work harder, you tell me it will take longer?" the boy asked. "The answer is clear", the master said, "When one eye is fixed upon your destination, there is only one eye left with which to find the Way."[7]

So, too much focus on the destination, no time to enjoy the way! There is little doubt that leaders-with-an-eye-or-two-on-the-journey deal with powerful and rich elements of the organization's life. We talk of a long journey or a difficult or a challenging one. We talk about what we find, what we miss,

---

[7] Hyams, Joe, 1990, *Zen in The Martial Arts*, Bantam Doubleday Dell Publishing, New York

what we lose, who is coming with us. We recount anecdotes, tales, stories. We have memories of the journey, sometimes written, others verbal or even graphical.

▶ What do you mean, it's muddy?

Moses was a journey-leader! Come with me to the land of milk and honey! So they went, it took a little while to arrive, there was no milk, there was no honey. But the journey created the nation of Israel (with the help of Egypt). A cartoon I love is one of Moses on top of a hill with the Red Sea waters parted in front of him and an incredulous multitude below, not knowing exactly what to make of it. Part of the crowd is looking at the water and another part at Moses himself. And a very irritated Moses shouts: "*What do you mean, it's muddy?*"

Journey-leaders in my experience are a bit like Moses, half puzzled, half cross that followers may not see the journey as a good idea! But to them, the journey is the vision! A beautiful poem by Spanish poet Antonio Machado reads:

> *Walker, there is no road.*
> *The road is made as you walk.*
> *As you walk the road is made*
> *and when you look behind you*
> *you see the trail*
> *you will never step on again.*[8]

---

[8] Machado, Antonio (1875 – 1939). *Walker, there is no road (Caminante, no hay camino)*

▶ One way tickets

Some leaders are good at moving forward, with more or less an idea of destinations and with (more or less) good maps, but certainly with one fixed intention: there is no u-turn. It may be the business circumstances or a personal style, but these leaders never go back. It is only forward that matters. These are Cortés leaders (Hernán Cortés burnt his ships when he arrived in Mexico as a conquistador). Other leaders play backwards and forwards, more like chess players. Which one's good and which one bad? As in any other of the seven faces of the leader, that's not the question. The question is what type are you, what do you project, and what are the consequences for the organization?

Maps, destination and journeys are the trio in this face of the leader. Imagine the following 'leadership styles' (within this face):

- A destination, no maps, incredible journey.
- Maps, no clear destination, keep moving, we'll find it ("*it will become clear*").
- Journey, journey, journey, this is the destination.
- Destination and map and journey, here is the whole package.

or possibly, other combinations! There is no question that leadership is different depending on how you treat the three components. I suggest that it is now your turn to reflect, to look at yourself in the mirror, make some sense of it all and plan, perhaps, for practicing more the dimensions that you have overlooked or the ones that you have never thought about.

Questions

Maps, destinations and journeys are the three dimensions here. Let's recap and reflect upon them via 'questions'. This is my suggested list, but it will never be complete until you add your own questions.

- Use the list to trigger new questions or to attempt to answer them! Make notes, use the book!
- Commit to one single step to 'answer the question'. These steps may look like actions you want to take, questions you want to ask other people in your organization or 'practice' that you want to do at your next opportunity.

Maps

- Do I allow for irrationality? What degree?
- Do I always lead in pre-determined pathways or allow for some sort of 'pathway finding'?
- Do I provide 'maps'? What do they look like? Are they satellite maps or street maps, high level or detailed?
- Does it matter how those maps are received by people who depended upon me or follow me?
- How much of cause-effect do my maps contain?
- As a leader, am I prepared to challenge some rationality in favour of alternatives?
- How much of psychological 'training' or self-development am I putting in place to understand many 'irrational behaviours' in my organization? Or do I try

to dismiss them as undesirable or irrelevant because they would not lead us to pre-determined destinations?

- What kind of 'maps' do we have in our organization?
- If we have vision statements, missions, quality sets, credos, leadership behaviours, change management frameworks, how good are they as maps?
- How are people using them? Do we use them as 'maps' or as fixed-benign-dictatorship type of control?
- Who owns these 'maps' in our organizations? Management? HR?
- Do you have too many? Are you inducing initiative fatigue?

Destinations

- Am I a fixed-destination leader or aspiring to be one? Is fixed destination the only possibility that would make me comfortable?
- Am I/ would I be uncomfortable with exploring 'terra incognita'?
- When I explain 'vision' to people, do I do so that in terms of 'place of arrival', direction to follow or way to move forward, or combinations?
- What's my personal dose of mixture of the three that I can live with?
- Are you a 'keep walking', a 'lets have more data first', or both, sort of leader. Would you be embarrassed to say, *"let's move, we'll find out"*?
- Are you in rehearsal mode (preparing for later) or living this life?
- Where do you look for your keys when you lose them? Do you take people with you where there is more light or do you venture with them into dark places?

- Find some examples where in the past you or your organization have only been 'looking for keys where there is more light'. It would be very interesting if you and your team analyse this.

Journeys

- Do you care about 'the journey' or the way?
- Or are you a destination-at-all-cost leader? Does it matter?
- Could you describe the journey to your people?
- Could you imagine, picture the journey?
- Could you conceive the journey itself as a leadership objective?
- Are you Cortés, burning ships? Is chess playing a better model for you?
- What are the consequences of these 'styles'?

ACTION MAP
(some first pass questions)

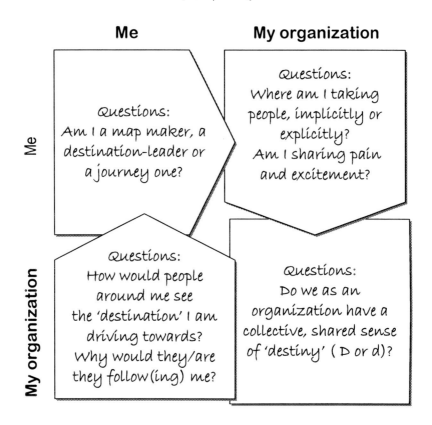

Me　　　　　　　　**My organization**

Me

Questions:
Am I a map maker, a
destination-leader or
a journey one?

Questions:
Where am I taking
people, implicitly or
explicitly?
Am I sharing pain
and excitement?

My organization

Questions:
How would people
around me see
the 'destination' I am
driving towards?
Why would they/are
they follow(ing) me?

Questions:
Do we as an
organization have a
collective, shared sense
of 'destiny' (D or d)?

This is a very simple set of questions to get you started
with your reflections and actions. Use the blank pages to
record your own questions and notes

▶ *Your Questions and Notes:*

▶ *Your Questions and Notes:*

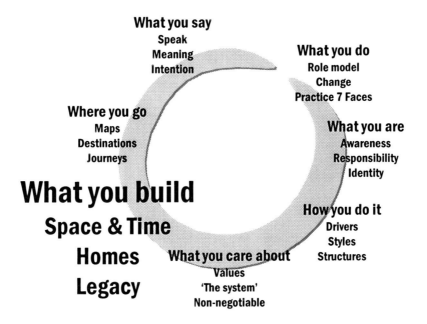

What you say
Speak
Meaning
Intention

What you do
Role model
Change
Practice 7 Faces

Where you go
Maps
Destinations
Journeys

What you are
Awareness
Responsibility
Identity

What you build
Space & Time
Homes
Legacy

How you do it
Drivers
Styles
Structures

What you care about
Values
'The system'
Non-negotiable

The Leader with Seven Faces

3   What you build
Time and Space
Homes
Legacy

We shape our buildings and afterwards they shape us
Winston Churchill[9]

From the multiple tasks, duties and roles expected, ascribed to or desired from the 21st century business leader, there is one that I would put well above anything else. Certainly well above the pursuit of shareholder value, market leadership, company growth, new product development, innovation, long term vision, attraction of talent, making it to the most-admired-corporation list, provide direction, assemble the best possible team, master globalization, create the best customer service in the world, 'flawless execution', 'customer intimacy', inspiration-for-all and walking on water.

The ultimate responsibility of the 21st century leader of any small company, big company, small division, big division, small team, big team is the protection of time and the creation of 'spaces'.

---

[9] Churchill, Winston, 1943, Quote from speech to the House of Commons

93

▶ *A special kind of architect*

This face of the leader is the face of an architect. In this conversation, I'd like to explore with you three dimensions of this architecture:

- **Time and Space:** good leaders build them, bad leaders destroy them! These are precious assets for the organization.

- **Homes:** what leaders build (ideas, purposes, dreams, ventures, teams, adventures, companies, futures…) produces a sense of belonging in people. Leaders build 'homes' for human capital, for relationships (social capital) and for 'ways of doing' (organizational capital). Organizations may 'contain' projects, initiatives, talent, ideas, but these may be homeless.

- **Legacy:** this is the ultimate test of leadership. What leaders leave behind does matter. What we inherit from leaders - whether they are business, political, religious or social ones - has a direct impact on all of us. Unfortunately, this is one of those dimensions better explored a posteriori! Good leaders are conscious of their legacy all the time because they project and imagine a future.

Time

"It is time, stupid!" is how the much-needed campaign slogan would read. Time is man's last asset. Perception of time is in part personal and in part cultural. Some people's mind is of the 'we-have-plenty-of-time-for' type and others' is of the 'there-is-no-time-for' type. Both may be looking at exactly the same issue, the same timetable, the same facts! These differences are well-rooted in our brains and differentiate us, one from the other. There are also big trans-cultural East-West differences although neo-global-capitalism is homogenizing the business world and global executives start to look alike.

Time is elusive. We have been taught that we have to make 'efficient use of time' but we are not sure what exactly that means other than being able to do what needs to be done! In the old days, we used to send our managers to time management courses. I have been invited (forced?) to attend several of these in my previous business life and always ended up with a new filofax, daytimer or other kind of binder.

▶ Individual concepts of time

The fundamental flaw of those courses - both the old ones and the new electronic-world ones - is that they assume there's a universal best way of managing a supposedly universal time-control-and-efficiency problem. They work for many people, don't get me wrong. But they do not account for the individualized 'concept of time'. For example, it is possible to dissect the day into bits and allocate them to, let's say 'meetings'. But it would be more difficult to universally distribute the time between let's say 'time to do' and 'time to think'. The latter is tricky because we all differ in the way we do it.

For many people, the simple dictation *"now, stop and think"* is a recipe for mental block. For these people, 'thinking' (about new ideas, new angles, possibilities of tackling A or B, solving X or Y, my next steps) is something that happens all the time. These people may have peaks of 'aha!' driving home, in the middle of the night, or whilst attending a conference on a topic miles away from the 'object of thinking'. Other people seem to grab - with both hands! - the chance of a pre-scheduled afternoon dedicated to non-operational worries. It is part of our own personal and professional development to figure out what works best for us and - once we figured it out - to try to develop mechanisms to do what I have called 'protect time'.

▶ Protecting time

I am not calling it 'creating time' because time is already there, we just need to 'see it' and protect it from all the physical and psychological invasions. Physically protecting time may look like a 'close the door' or 'don't come in' behaviour, if you can do it! Psychologically, it means to carve out your own 'space' to be able to – and here the terminology is very personal - reflect, think, ponder etc. As above, those who 'can't do that' - because the simple constraint of pre-scheduled-time-to-think-and-reflect would block them from thinking and reflecting - but who are still in need of doing so (and, incidentally, have back-to-back meetings in Outlook until 2023), have to learn to create those spaces. Period. Part of leadership development is to be able to become architects of those spaces, for oneself and the organization behind.

For many, the initial confrontation with 'free time' may look scary above all! But there is no other trick. Practice! In a recent seminar that I ran, I met somebody who disclosed to us that he organizes 'fake projects' in his Outlook calendar and project-manages them accordingly. This is the only way to ensure that his time is not cannibalized by the thousand and one ways of time being used and commoditized in the organization!

▶ Managed by my calendar

Life in many organizations today looks like devolution of responsibility to Mr Microsoft Outlook. Outlook is in charge. (Apologies to the three or four other souls, users of alternative systems!) It is the real boss. We may kid ourselves by thinking that it is a tool but, in reality, we do report to it, which automatically makes Bill Gates our boss. Scary thought. 'Managing my calendar' has become a management term, de facto making the *calendar* and *you* one single entity. I am I and my Outlook.

As I mentioned above, it is no longer a joke that people 'can't find gaps in their calendar' for many months in advance. Whatever you think of busy business life, it tells us a lot about the kind of organizations that we are developing, perhaps the one you are working for. I believe that time is man's last asset. If this is true, and you have been booked until five p.m. on Wednesday 23 May 2016, you, my friend, have no assets left whatsoever and are mentally bankrupt.

►*Always-on leader*

Meet Michèle. Born in France, she is a successful senior executive in an American company and has been living in the UK for the last five years. She is married to an Englishman, has no children, one big dog and a large country house close enough to Heathrow airport. She is first-and-last in the car park (first to arrive, last to leave) like a punctuality check for the security staff – *"if this is Michèle, it must be 7 o'clock"*. Because of the time difference with the USA, when she gets home, Michèle connects to her email system via the company-paid home broadband.

Evening glass of wine in hand, she often picks up the phone to talk to an American colleague if she sees something on screen that needs addressing soon. When travelling, she uses, of course, her mobile phone and her wireless laptop. She has just bought a Blackberry, so flow of email is more or less 'all the time/always on'. She uses all possible wi-fi spots in airport lounges or wireless internet in hotel rooms. The days of dealing with obscure continental telephone sockets are over. Connection with the web is almost automatic. She uses her voicemail system several times a day. Michèle has staff reporting to her in Germany and France and a boss in San Francisco. The latter likes to call her at 'any time'. Michèle's mobile is never switched off – it is not the number of calls from her boss (not many, to be fair) but the necessary feeling of 'just in case'.

Michèle is a case of a 365/24/7 connected employee. She is an always-on executive. Her husband, an IT manager, told her once that she was in reality an 'extension of the network'. Michèle's contract says something about 38 hours a week but she is in fact working for her company 'all the time'. She is part of a tribe of global managers with an unofficial, unwritten 365-days-a-year commitment who are 'permanently on call'. Whether in the middle of cooking fettuccini or in the bath, Michèle is 'never disconnected'. Her favourite verbal stereotype is "*I have no time.*" She usually means she is in a hurry but, in reality, the statement is actually a pure representation of her reality. She literally has *NO* time. She does not possess it anymore. She is part of an era described by Jacob Needleman, professor of Philosophy at San Francisco University, as 'the time famine'.[10] Michèle has given up her most valuable asset. Her last.

▶ *21ˢᵗ Century presenteeism*

We all know one Michèle or two. Perhaps she is you? Forget all that stuff about work/life balance. The Michèles of this world have an all-in-one package. Corporations have reinvented 'presenteeism' (the old insistence that you must be at your desk, every day, clock-checked, etc.) in the form of a '365/24/7 on call, online, wireless, Blackberry, real-time manager'. In fact, for many senior managers, there is no longer the expectation of a nine-to-five physical presence at the office and the 'rules' have been 'relaxed' (!) or replaced with occasional or, indeed, pre-agreed working-from-home days. Nine–to-five is no longer a good sign of commitment. 24h-open- shop is. What is largely perceived as liberation is nothing more than a sophisticated form of dependence. Place has been traded off for time. The company office or module

---

[10] Needleman, Jacob, 1998, *Time and The Soul*, Bantam Double Day Dell Publishing, New York

has been traded off for a mobile telephone, a Blackberry and a fast internet access line at home.

Far be it from me to draw a picture here of malicious corporations with Machiavellian plans for a slave workforce, a subtle form of 24h control of people's lives, written down by the Board in a secret black book. If there is any guilt at all, it is three-fold: employers, employees and the nature of the Information Era.

In the current knowledge economy, it is difficult to escape the multi-task, multi-assignment, any-place, any-time job. Technology allows us to be 'anywhere'. Emails have brought an 'end-of-distance' to our desks. They bring to you instant data, and ask you for an instant answer from your instant knowledge pool (whilst you are probably drinking instant coffee). It is real-time business, a '24 hour society'. To be a successful manager progressing towards a bigger corporate destiny has become incompatible with a nine-to-five job or, indeed, a Monday to Friday one.

Airports on Sunday afternoons are full of executive-like faces with their proverbial suit carriers, ready to fly for a Monday morning meeting somewhere far away. Michèle does that. An additional problem is that she had not *realized* that fact until a colleague asked her recently to spend a few minutes on her own calendar. Michèle's perception was: *"Leaving on a Sunday evening? I do it occasionally."* In reality, for the previous six months, she had hardly had a full weekend at home. 'Insight' went out of the window in the company of 'time'.

There is a real danger for organizations today to allow or promote the progressive evolution towards an entire always-on managerial and leadership class. Time-less leaders will be no good to anybody, corporations or families. When there is no time to think, there is no time for being. Time-less leaders are *doing* all the time, they have no time for *being*. If it sounds a bit New Age, so be it! Intelligent corporations, large or small, deserve intelligent leaders. Intelligent leaders will have to encourage the protection of employees' time as opposed to the absorption and further commoditization of their last remaining asset. The more they act to protect a sort of endangered species, the more they will benefit from people with a functional brain who are actually capable of using their minds, as opposed to logarithmically multiplying the email traffic and skilfully contribute to the internal information pollution of the company. There is still time. Isn't there?

▶ *Fast ethos*

A consequence of the 'no time' ethos is the 'fast ethos". There is no time, so you have to run fast, be agile, be first, etc. Society, and therefore business, is working on a 'time-space compression'. The American driven fast-food industry has known it for a long time. As it has been expressed, they have *"taught us to eat standing, walking, running and driving and above all never to finish a meal, all in favour of the endless snack"*. Eating has been reduced to *"a purely instrumental, no-nonsense utilitarian activity which exemplifies a 're-fuelling ethos', rather than an intrinsic source of pleasure to be anticipated"*. No wonder the 'Slow Food movement' became a truly international one!

The 'fast ethos' goes hand in hand with the 'ephemeral ethos' that takes for granted that things will not last. It is a common feature in fast-cycle businesses where products become obsolete quickly, but it has also been extrapolated to the ethos of the entire new, 21st century enterprise. We all have friends somewhere who have started their own company with the idea of selling it as soon as possible. Most of the ones I know, do not intend to stay with their own baby for long.

Venture capitalists and investors have long incorporated the 'exit' aspect as central to the deal. How to *exit* is as important as how to *enter*, and it is part of written business plans. I know of somebody who could not give me the name of his new company but had already thought out the 'exit'. He is a young guy for whom this is *the* normal way to set up business. He did not know of any other, and looked at me puzzled at my suggestion of creating something that could last 'forever'.

▶ *The end of time*

A quick Amazon.com search will tell you that there are 800+ book titles which start with 'The end of'. Affluence, man, distance, work, politics, nature, sanity, the future, ideology, capitalism are some of them. From those, there are more than twenty recent ones entitled *The end of Time*. This lot includes slow-digestion physics books sharing shelf space with more dubious 'time management books', which are an industry of its own. It's funny to see what lives on the same shelf!

This 'End of Everything' may just reflect the fact that things have changed at an unprecedented pace, producing quantum discontinuity. In this accelerated time, fast is good, slow is suicidal. The fanciest business magazine is called *Fast Company*. *Business Week*, referring to the new start-up companies, announced a few years ago that it takes on average 10 days from idea to business plan and launch. It used to be months. Today, perhaps it's an afternoon. Venture capitalists tell us that *"whilst it used to be that the big eat the small, now the fast eats the slow"*. 'Speed' is considered the new revered capability, a crossroads for new corporate competencies that include 'surprise'.

This connection of *no-time/ephemeral organization/run fast in the meantime* has profound implications on the reflection of your leadership style. Don't expect a prescription from this book, but perhaps you have never stopped and reflected upon this (Ooops! I see, you can't stop, you don't have time, hum!).

Here are two different views on speed:

John Chambers, President and CEO of Cisco Systems, Inc.:

"Companies that are successful will have cultures that thrive on change, even though change makes most people very uncomfortable. In the end, you might just have speed, talent and branding. Those things may be the only differentiators"

Note speed first in the list! Now meet Andy Grove, ex-CEO of Intel:

"This business about speed has its limits. Brains don's speed up. The exchange of ideas does not really speed up, only the overhead that slowed down the exchange. When it comes down to the bulk of knowledge work, the 21st century works

the same as the 20th century. You can reach people around the clock, but they won't think any better or any faster just because you've reached them faster. The give and take remains a limiting factor."

What I find interesting about those quotations from public statements is that they come from two leader executives of hi-tech industries, certainly involved in … making information flow faster, to say the least. They represent two legitimate views of the (business) world. What 'side' leaders take matters because, as architects, the houses they build will be a reflection of their concepts of time and speed.

Space

As a leader, the protection of time is intimately related to the creation of 'space' and possibly 'place'. Space and Place are not the same. Space is mainly psychological. It gives people the ability to make the most of their 'being' by stop 'doing'. People can work in a big place, like a big office, and have absolutely no space. All space and time may have been swallowed by Outlook, for example! Other people may work in not-very-big places and still enjoy (psychological) space.

As leader, a possible trap to avoid is to declare universal ways to create those spaces, the equivalent of telling somebody, *"It is Thursday afternoon, have your space, think*!" What leaders need to do is to be sensitive to our diversity and allow or create opportunities for a somehow tailored approach. However, 'generic measures' may work as a symbolic behaviour. Statistically, they may also reduce the amount of 'trapped time and space' for people. Some of them may look terribly simple such as a rule that says, *"Do not reply to any email unless you are the main recipient"*. That would exclude all replies in 'cc' and 'bcc'situations. Some organizations have tried 'no meetings on Friday' for example or 'email server down' for fixed dedicated hours. People may have a bit of laugh about these but sometimes this is the only way to instil new behaviours.

If you live a corporate life – corporate of a certain size, that is – you may have experienced the nuisance of 'the server is down' at some point. It starts as a small irritation because it is implicit that it will be solved soon by the IT department. The irritation grows enormously when this is not the case. Three hours later you are told that, in reality, you have a serious problem and it may take far longer than expected. Suddenly, people around you start looking relaxed!

There is a strong case for breakdown-time-by-design! The contagious beneficial effect of these otherwise simplistic micro-management measures is that people realize that, contrary to expectations, the corporation doesn't go under, the sky doesn't fall, projects continue and one was not as indispensable as one may have thought. General De Gaulle was quoted to say that cemeteries are full of indispensable people! Significantly, email traffic does not increase or bounce back after the blackout period, and the number of meetings on Monday to Thursday does not increase either.

How each of us interprets, feels and 'uses' space is perhaps different and can't be imposed or dictated. You and I know people who seem to have 'no space', their constant 'doing' occupies their life. We also know other people who seem to manage to 'protect themselves' from the corrosion of nonstop-doing. When in my leadership seminars I ask people to reflect upon their own mechanisms and 'label them', they come up with long and in many cases amusing lists. Here is an example:

Just-give-me-Space
Inner space
Space-Space
Time-space
Think-space
Break space
Parenthesis-Space
Outside Course-Space
Gone-Fishing-Space
Beer-Space
Awareness-Space
How-are-you-Space
Don't-push-me-Space
Embrace-silence-Space
Doing-nothing-Space

People describe their 'concepts of space' in multiple ways. In some cases it means to physically transplant oneself to a 'place' where psychological space can be felt and experienced. One executive described his 'gone-fishing-space', meaning, don't try, you'll not find me, that's it... Actually, he had never been fishing in his life but stole the concept from a movie where somebody stuck a sign outside the shop window. He liked the idea so much that he has used the 'gone fishing' since. Beyond the light idea and language that he used, what he portrayed was a genuine sense of a need to protect his individuality and 'disappear'.

Another executive who described her 'how-are-you-space', told us (the group attending the seminar) that her daily business life did not have a moment for, what she described as, *"a normal conversation with a normal person."* (Obviously she must have had a particular view of the normality of her business colleagues!). For her, the protection of her space, her individuality and her being meant almost the opposite of 'gone-fishing'. In fact, her space creation and protection was about engaging herself with other (normal!) people in conversations that she qualified as 'real life'. And that had to be done outside the office!

► *Social space*

Mothers are very often trapped in a vicious circle of child-feeding, nappy-changing and sleepless nights (My general practitioner says to them, *"YOU will understand why sleep deprivation is barred under the Geneva Convention"*). They are a good example of always-doing-not-much-time-for-being. Sometimes this period of their life becomes a-social (!) with baby-talk occupying much of daily airtime. Their need for 'space' is often translated not into need for sleep, isolation and tranquillity (although those are, of course, also very welcome!) as you would have expected, but the opposite: opportunity to talk to other adults, socialize and recover a sense of connection with the world! As in the previous example, their space creation is social, not a 'gone-fishing' one, because that social space makes them 'feel human' again.

Also, people mistake this issue with the famous 'work-life balance'. It is often assumed by people that a work-intensive environment with not much flexibility for those protections

---

must surely be compensated by a non-work one full of 'space' and 'time'. (Watch the language! We call 'life' the other side of 'work' in the work-life balance, which says a lot about our concept of work.) But being trapped in an environment with perhaps reasonable 'place' but no 'space' and 'no' time is not exclusive to work. Family life with its commitments and challenges (and not only for mothers!) may equally be one of non-space, and the same principles apply. So, let's not get this wrong. Space is not necessarily about solitude!

I make no apologies for my insistence on the protection-of time-and-space despite the fact that, statistically, only some privileged managers, executives, leaders, employers or employees have access to mechanisms such as the ones that create or protect them. Many people are trapped in jobs and levels of freedom and autonomy where their flexibility to seek a protection of space is limited. If they read this, they would think that you and I - lucky fellows who could still craft some spaces of freedom - are…well, just lucky!

▶ Sitting quietly alone

The French philosopher Pascal said that "*all of humanity's problems stem from man's inability to sit quietly in a room alone*". It is a valid statement today. Modern life, organizational life, business life is not terribly conducive to letting ourselves be with ourselves 'in a room alone'. But the need to find that 'lost space' is greater than ever.

All this stuff about psychological spaces and protection of time will also sound incredible stupid to the always-on executive, the one who never switches off. As Michèle's husband says, this kind of leader and the company's server are a continuum via a wireless umbilical cord recently called, amongst other names, Blackberry.

As leader, or leader-to-be, or leader in development.... you should look into all these issues seriously. Some people take a view that it is simply logistics, a question of good time management. Other people however tend to think that there is a more fundamental problem behind the pervasive and ubiquitous busy-ness of executive life.

There is little question that concepts of reality are different depending on what view you take. And - as I said in the introduction of this book and repeat in my Leadership seminars - the answers to these questions are personal. Unfortunately, the consequences of the answers are not.

As a leader who builds organizations (ideas projects, common purpose around a vision), how you choose to answer matters, not only to you but to everybody else depending on you. Not a minor burden.

▶ *I never heard the builders!*

Constantine P. Cavafy, a poet who died in 1933, wrote a little poem called *Walls*. This is how it goes:

> *Walls*
>
> *With no consideration, no pity, no shame,*
> *they have built walls around me, thick and high.*
> *And now I sit here feeling hopeless.*

*I can't think of anything else: this fate gnaws my mind,
because I had so much to do outside.
When they were building the walls, how could I not
have noticed!
But I never heard the builders, not a sound.
Imperceptibly they have closed me off from the outside
world.*

Many people in our organizations reach late age surrounded
by walls (their own career pathways, the single track pursuit
of success, the 365/24/7 busy-ness as leader), only to realize
that there are walls around when it is too late. Those people
will shout, *"But I never heard the builders! I was doing my
emails on my Blackberry and there was nothing in Outlook
about any walls of any kind. Did I miss a meeting about
walls? What's happened to me? Julia! (calling his last PA)
Julia!"* Julia can't answer. She is not deaf but those walls are
so thick!

▶ Those who hear the builders

People who leave an organization do so for a variety of
reasons. One of them is sometimes the feeling that 'the walls'
are getting thicker and taller. They realize at some point that
their personal or professional development requires that they
push themselves outside those walls. In some cases, it means
the next job, next context. In many cases, it means to start a
business on their own. In the last decades, there has been an
explosion of people 'going solo', 'liberating themselves' from
corporate life, 'becoming their own boss', etc. This has been
particularly noticeable in the US. There is a healthy,
entrepreneurial, adventurous side of this that fits very well in

the traditional 'American dream', in whatever version there is these days. But there is also a sad side for 'the company'.

▶ 100k investment lost

It has always surprised me. Corporations are resigned to let their best entrepreneurs go on the grounds that it is normal for those people to want to exit corporate life. They are not good at dealing with many practices and procedures, hate too much reporting, need an agile 'entrepreneurial environment', want to be more free, to make decisions that matter and to feel that they can see the differences they make. So they have to go! Great! So we acknowledge that rigidity, over-reporting, lousy decisions and lack of freedom are an inevitable part of corporate life.

If a £2000 laptop is missing from the office, we will launch an investigation. If an entrepreneur leaves to create his own show because he can't stand the constraints of the company, we call it natural fact of life. I heard this comment many years ago and it's still valid today. How interesting! Instead of fixing the internal rigidity problems we prefer to let human capital go in search of a more motivating environment. We will even have a party to say goodbye and celebrate the loss. Accountants will be happier because they have just made a saving on the balance sheet. It's the surreal world of management: let somebody go and you'll save money.

It is probably impossible to pretend that the entire culture, systems and processes of a medium-sized or big company changes overnight to accommodate for entrepreneurial groups on the inside, but can we do anything about it? Yes, we can!

Provided that the leadership is not too scared to 'allow' different operating structures to cohabit within the firm, that there is no obsession with uniformity of systems and that the focus is to make the most of those entrepreneurs at the gates (that is, in this case, entrepreneurs about to get out), there are definitely ways.

I bring this topic here as an example of leader's architecture designed to create space and place for people. And this is far from altruistic. It is an example most applicable to medium or large organizations but the principles would be more universally valid. I am talking here about self-contained, entrepreneurial 'business units' within a large organization that can be designed to take advantage of the large company context, but without its bureaucratic liability, and with the attraction of the small 'independent' organization. They live a symbiotic life with the company, and somewhere else I have called them 'SymBUnits', that is symbiotic business units. They are inside the firm. Individuals don't have to open the gates and go… but they are different from the rest. And here are the differences:

1. **Protected boundaries**. The borders of the unit, the group of individuals or the 'special team', must be protected (by management) but those borders may be permeable. Actually, they may even look more like Monaco borders than Heathrow borders. When in Monte Carlo, you have to look hard to see any visible difference from France other than the police hats. But they have their own police, banking system, laws and government. Some of these groups of entrepreneurs-inside-the-gates may be similar, separated more by an osmotic membrane than a rigid organization chart. But

don't be fooled, accountability and clarity of goals will be there. Yes, some degree of ambiguity may be necessary, and this is not everybody's cup of tea.

These units need to be particularly good at stakeholder management and at nurturing their interfaces with the rest of the organization. They may need resources in and out, part-time people lent from other parts of the company, and a mixture of secondments and fixed headcount, all in one. Today's structure may look different tomorrow. They may represent a bit of a moving target for HR departments! But the leadership needs to protect that permeability and those semi-invisible borders to facilitate a sense of identity.

2. **Clear, well-defined output intent**. These groups must have a clear idea of what they are going to deliver in return for their protected uniqueness. Of course, their delivery must add value. Expectations must be clearly defined and those expectations must be aligned with their special charter, which, incidentally, must be well documented and shared.

3. **Operating model freedom**. These units must be free to operate in a different way from the rest of the organization. Within the agreed charter and their permeable boundaries, they must have protected freedom to establish their own processes and sit outside the homogeneity of the rest of the firm. They make their own rules. They should not be forced to follow the same systems and procedures as anybody else. If there is a massive, corporate, overall project management system with defined reporting and

control, for example, they must be allowed to opt out if it's not suitable. There is no point to give them the borders, charters and protection and pretend that they will behave like anybody else. If project teams report monthly to management, these units may want to do it weekly or quarterly. That can be agreed upfront, of course, but the whole point of having them is that they can enjoy a more agile, fast-track, tailored way of doing things. This is particularly worrying to command and control bosses.

4. **Resource control**. Within the agreed framework, these intrapreneurial groups must fully control their allocated resources, with direct visible accountability of their use. They must be free to outsource if needed. They should be allowed to spend the money in the way they need, not the way the rest of the organization does. Scary again, but, yet, what's the point of having them following the same rules? At this point of my presentation, I usually get things such as: "*Oh my God, this is crazy, a recipe for chaos.*" But it is not, if you trust them enough to allow their set-up.

5. **Magnet for talent**. These 'units' must by design be magnets for talent inside the firm (and outside). They must exhibit an ability to seduce and attract the best hearts and minds. These units must pride themselves to become 'the place to be', a prestige, elite space where growing intellectual capital is as easy as growing mushrooms (in places where mushrooms grow!) Inevitably, you are creating some sort of internal competition, but this is healthy. The role of other parts of the organization is to become 'the place

to be' themselves as well, not to complain about unfair treatment or differentiation. There is no law that says that you have to run parts of the organization that must be defined as 'the places not to be'. If there are lousy processes and boring work, these have been created by man. Man can change that.

6. **High Brokerage skills**. Although brokerage is part of normal leadership, these 'units' must be exquisite at that capability, They will have to constantly negotiate with other parts of the organization to protect their boundaries, use ad hoc resources, and make trade-offs. Their leader is their Master Broker. The leader of these units must be unapologetically contagious in his or her energy, determination and passion. Passion is not necessarily jumping in the corridor singing and clapping – business passion is a deep belief in what one is doing (when in doubt, look at your entrepreneur friends who left, passing through those open gates).

7. **Identity and destiny**. And now it gets even more philosophical (and scarier for standard managers). These units must have a sense of 'any-size-d' destiny, as I mentioned in chapter 1. I don't mind whether you use a big D or small d, but sense of destiny means that they share a good awareness of their potential unique impact on the organization. They want to be remembered as 'the ones who did such and such, who developed that product, who created that new idea, who commercialized that opportunity, etc'. People in these intrapreneurial cells have a high sense of belonging. The unit is their reference place. They are

aware of their elite status and all the benefits and the liabilities associated with it.

8. **Knowledge incubation.** These units thrive on knowledge creation, sharing and transfer. They invest heavily on training and development of their people on anything that is necessary even if it's not part of the training portfolio available in the company. If somebody needs to be trained on something specific that is desperately needed, here you go, here is the ticket and the credit card, go and get it. They take intellectual leadership seriously and pay a lot of attention to their own recycling of skills and capabilities. Incidentally, they control their training budget, the one that usually gets cut around September time when the company needs to make some 'savings to compensate for the lower than expected sales in Singapore' and/or the 'unfavourable currency conversion'.

9. **Urgency ethos.** They have a culture sense of urgency. Sense of urgency is not synonymous of all-fast-at-any-cost. They have a motto: "*Life is short*". They protect their 'time to think' but then, it's all go. They politely answer the concerns about quality by professing quality as a given, as a 'pass', as a baseline, not as an aim in itself. Whilst other people produce quality ideas, quality products, quality services and quality goods for the sake of quality, they produce them for the sake of the output itself, their added value, which just happens to have high quality. Quality is a given, slowness is not negotiable. As I mentioned in the previous chapter - referring to 'the tyranny of the or'-

many people around them say that it's one or the
other, quality or speed, one compromises the other,
they can't have it both ways. To which they respond,
"Watch me!"

10. **Emergent architecture**. Over time, the shape of the
SymBUnits, intrapreneurial units, in-venture groups or
whatever you may choose to call them, may change.
The composition of members, nature of their network,
size of the operation, etc. may evolve. However, the
foundations remain.

You have noticed that I have been calling these groups
differently all the time. This is by design because it is not a
question of creating a new 'theory of the organization' or 'a
new model' but applying the principles no matter what form,
shape or label. Structural evolution in these groups follows
more of a self-organising path than a designed plan. Identity
remains high all the time, but the borders of those Monacos
may look like a moving target.

The old Arab choice between having enemies inside the tent
but pissing out (annoying) or having them outside the tent but
pissing in (more annoying), also applies here. Choosing
between all those about-to-leave people (going outside the
tent and eventually pissing in) and creating an inside-the-tent
strategy (definitely far more hygienic) that keeps talent in the
organization… Well, it's your choice. You will also introduce
healthy internal competition. These 'structures' are ideal for
internal ventures, fast-track development projects, expansions
into new fields, special projects, one-stop problem solving
'teams', internal product incubators, hosts for different

product-development life cycles inside the same organization, or just intrapreneurial pockets retaining talent.

I am told that on the door of a GE facility in India there is a sign: 'Trespassers will be recruited'. You as leader should have an equivalent sign for your organization, perhaps something along the lines of 'Leavers will be recruited again.'

Homes

Leaders build 'homes'. Leaders build organizational I.Q. which is a combination of three things:

- **Human Capital:** the combination of individual talents, assets that the company does not possess but hosts. The organization is like an investment bank using other people's talent(s).

- **Social capital:** the quantity and quality of relationships between people internally and externally and between the organization and other organizations.

- **Architectural capital:** the assets developed and grown from (a) a particular 'way of doing things' and (b) a particular way of being organized.

▶ *The no-war on talent*

In 1997, McKinsey-consultants coined the term 'war on talent' to describe the fight between corporations over the attraction of good human capital. Talent is a key asset, not a commodity, so there must be a war to win it for the company. There were articles and more articles and a book… It took a few years for somebody to shine a different light on the problem and, as in many cases before, it was Prof Jeffrey Pfeffer of Stanford University who did it. I learnt of this through an intriguing article in the Financial Times in 2001 with the title *The futile war on talent*. After all the noise made about the war, to have the FT saying there wasn't one, or that it was futile, deserved a bit of attention.

The thesis was very simple. All this business about a war on talent distracts people from focusing on the talent inside their organizations. By making so much noise about a talent that seems to be 'out there' and for which organizations are murdering each other, we lose sight of our own internal talent pool. The issue, the article put forward, was how to host talent (whether home-grown or attracted) not how to grab it from some sort of extra-terrestrial place.

▶ *The investors metaphor*

Hosting talent is developing the organization's human capital. One of the roles of the leaders-architects is to build good hosts and hubs of something that they do not own: the individual's talent. Nobody has put it better than Thomas O. Davenport[11] with his 'investor metaphor' of workers. Employees were once treated as 'cost', then as 'most valuable assets' and now they should be seen – he says- as investors, that is, investors

---

[11] Davenport, Thomas O., 1999, *Human Capital: What it is and Why people invest it*, Josse-Bass Inc., San Fransisco

of their own human capital. It is a very interesting concept from the leadership perspective.

What do you do when you invest? You go and find a place where your capital is going to grow! At the end of the year, or whatever other period, you are going to compare what you put in and what you got out! It follows that people should go and work at places where their human capital is going to grow, and where, in the process, it's being used by the organization. In this model, leaders are more like investment fund managers, creating the conditions for the growth. As such, they should be measured by their ability to show the growth. And this is a tricky one because whilst we are good at managing tangible assets, we're not necessarily that good at managing intangible ones. If your people are not sure about what 'intangible' means, use this:

A rich American lady visits the most famous hat maker in Paris. She sees a beautiful, exquisite, long ribbon and immediately falls in love. The hat maker takes the ribbon in his hands, does a few twists with it and creates a stunning hat. Brilliant! The lady grabs it immediately. *"How much is it?"* she asks. *"Five thousand Euros"*, the hat maker says. *"Five thousand Euros!"* the lady exclaims, *"But, it's just a ribbon!"* *"Madam"*, the hat maker says, *"the ribbon is free."*

▶ Collaborations

The second form of capital in the organizational I.Q. is social capital. This is the asset created by relationships, both internal and external, both in quantity and quality. The modern business organization of today has a web of external connections. Alliances, partnerships, joint-ventures etc. are common. The web may be so vast that it is bound to contain 'nodes' where competitors sit. Companies may find themselves competing and collaborating at the same time. It has been called co-opetition. Internally, organizations are rich in connections and relationships but most of the time they are ignorant, focusing only on a relatively small part of human collaboration models: the teams. I have called the current business organization a *teamocracy* because this model of collaboration has become coterminous with 'organization'.

In today's business organization, the organization chart is dead. The job description is dead. But, as of Mark Twain's, the death of the *structure* may have been grossly exaggerated. For clues, see Biology.

Like biological organisms, business organizations are in continuous adaptation to stimuli (external and internal environments), and must change and evolve accordingly. Biological organisms do not understand one year budget cycles, quarterly reporting on activity, one-off post-retreat reorganizations, static organization charts, two-page-forever job descriptions, or annual objectives set up in January and assessed in December. They grow, generate antibodies, move, reproduce, get smaller or bigger, and die at different paces and rhythms.

Their 'ultimate structure' is created by their functionality "*The function creates the organ*", I learnt from my anatomy teacher. Also, they can not be fully explained without reference to another system to which they belong or are connected to. In fact, they are *complex systems* that are better understood through the glasses of complexity theory.

Organizations may be just the same. What happens inside them can't be tracked by the static organization chart and the job description manual. The different components (people, groups, teams, networks of influence and power, etc.) are linked by an information flow which is far from static. The organization *is* an information network. Leaders today need to understand this. Organization-chart-management - fiddling around with reporting, solid lines, dotted lines, any combination - is like grammar. It has to be right. But leaders should play their role in literature. Mistaking one for the other is not a good sign of leadership. Let's take a further look at this property of the organization to create its own connections, because if this is true, then leaders have to be aware and also lead this 'more invisible part'.

▶ Kauffman buttons

Stuart Kauffman, of the Santa Fe Institute (a world centre for the study of complexity), explains some of the mechanisms in the generation of networks in a metaphor about 'buttons and threads'[12]. Scatter 20 buttons on a table, randomly choose two, connect them with threads and put them back. Repeat and repeat. At the beginning you are likely to choose buttons that are unconnected and that you have not picked up before, but, after a while, you will start picking up at random buttons that were already connected. Clusters of connected buttons will emerge.

---

[12] Kauffman, Stuart, 1995, *At home in the Universe – The Search for the laws of Self-organization and Complexity*, Oxford University Press, New York

A form of 'stable system' has been created from an apparently chaotic and random interaction. At the mid-point of this journey, when the ratio of threads to buttons is 0.5, the system experiences a 'phase transition' or *a sudden change in the size* of the largest connected cluster. Suddenly, you realize that you have a 'visible mass' in front of you. This is the 'transition point' when, for example, water freezes into ice.

Kauffman explains via simulation how, in a similar way, the 'interactions' of the total number of human genes gravitate to a smaller number of 'systems'. This is a number that - regardless of whether you are dealing with buttons and threads, genes, or any set of 'units' - tends to be pretty constant, roughly the square root of the number of original units. In the case of genes-to-cells, all the potential 'gene interactions' (for lack of a better way to describe them) do not generate a chaotic number of 'clusters': there is a definite number of known different types of cells in the human body.

The progression of genes-to-cells follows Kaufmann's 'order for free' mathematics, as in the buttons and threads case. It's a journey from chaos to stability, from something that seems like random or chaotic interactions to some sort of stable system: the ice from the water, the cells from the genes. Chaos and random connections do not seem to produce more chaos (which can be a consolation in one's life).

▶ *Leading an organization you can't see*

What does this have to do with organizations? Quite a lot... Individuals in organizations establish networks of interactions and communications. Some of them are 'official' and 'designed': teams, task forces, committees etc. It is the *teamocracy* part. But more interesting are the ones that may be formed like Kaufmanns's buttons: emergent clusters of individuals, not designed by the boss, but 'self-generated' by the interactions between them.

The literature describing 'non-designed' groups or associations inside the firm has become more and more solid in recent years. *Self-managed teams* are often interpreted in terms of semi-spontaneous associations that don't need a formal boss to achieve their objectives. The largely fallen-from-grace 'knowledge management' movement has created the term 'communities of practices' to describe networks of individuals linked by a common objective or interest (including the finding of solutions to an organizational problem). People following the systems approach and the concept of 'the learning organization', tend to refer to 'networks of commitment' with more emphasis on the mobilization of motivation and energy in the organization. 'Emergent teams' is another generic term frequently used. More on the spontaneity side, 'hot groups' have been described as mobilization of individuals with common interests and drivers of real organizational creativity. Finally, 'TeamNets' have been introduced in the UK as a 'way of encouraging voluntary relationships in team formation, information exchange and problem solving'.

All the above are examples of the richness of internal relationships within the organization, a form of capital waiting to be unleashed and constituting part of the social capital of the firm. The leader-architect role is one of facilitating, enhancing, promoting and fostering relationships. He has two choices: collaboration by design (teams, task forces) and emergent collaboration. The second is much scarier to lead!

What do all those 'emergent groups' have in common? Despite the different labels, probably a lot. For a start, they live outside the organization chart with different degrees of both independence and spontaneous formation. It may be that, like in Kaufman's buttons, they are somehow invisible at the beginning of their life and it is not until some level of interaction has been reached that they manifest themselves as a proper system. Leaders can no longer ignore 'the invisible world'!

▶ Creating associability

If these 'organizations within the organization' do exist (in the way the literature points to them), do they matter anyway? I suggest they do. The condition of 'associability' is perhaps one of the main sources of the so called 'social capital' of the firm. It is worth distinguishing between 'associability' and 'sociability'. Whilst 'sociability' has to do with the universal propensity to socialize, 'associability' is defined by the 'willingness and ability of individuals to subordinate personal goals and associated actions to collective goals and actions'. In other words, a sociable environment where people meet, discuss, interact and interchange communication is a prerequisite for 'associability', but does not necessarily lead to it; to the enormous added value of the 'association'.

The social capital of the firm is based upon internal and external relationships. It produces mutual benefits, for the individual and for the organization itself. It is an asset different from other forms of capital such as bricks-and-mortar (physical capital) or knowledge and technical ability of the individuals (human capital). As an asset, it must be managed like other types of capital. Volatile, short-term or superficial relationships will invariably also generate volatile and ephemeral social capital, or a so-called 'low social capital environment'. In these organizations, any form of leadership appeal for collective goals is a contradiction in terms. Individuals may get on with their jobs (as in their 'job descriptions'), and even do them well, but they may not be interested in anything else, certainly not in any form of collective collaboration that, in most cases, entails 'going the extra mile', beyond formal responsibilities. And it is in those circumstances where the real added value is generated and a real difference is made.

Robert Putman - a political scientist who has researched American social habits - discovered that, progressively, people are less inclined to join in collective activities, engage in communitarian projects, give money to charity etc. In other words, less donations, less voluntary work, less voting is converting American society – he says - into 'a nation of loners', where - and here's the metaphor - 'bowling alone'[13] has replaced league bowling.

Putman also refers to the concept of 'social capital' which he defines as 'connections between individuals, social networks and the norms of reciprocity and trustworthiness that arises from them'. When social capital is diminishing, something precious in the fabric of the civil society is disappearing.

---

[13] Putman, Robert, 2000, *Bowling Alone: The Collapse and Revival of American Community*, Simon&Schuster, New York

Is there a contradiction between Putman's findings in a society that, to him, is composed of members 'bowling alone' and organizational life in that same society, where a constant sermon about 'league bowling' (we are a team, we work as a team etc.) seems to dominate?

Is it possible that there are two societies: the nine-to-five of 'bowling together' and the five-to-nine and weekends of 'bowling alone'? Is Putman - by the very nature of his target research - ignoring that (professional) people spend most of their time 'at work', and therefore, bowling with others in the nine-to-five teamocracy"? Are we in a schizophrenic society? At the cynical end of the questions, could Putman be right and his 'bowling alone theory' be extended to the nine-to-five world? In other words, is the bowling together in the teamocracy just a superficial appearance whilst in the individual's heart he is still bowling alone?

▶ Bowling regardless? An organization of loners?

Putman's work made me think that perhaps many corporations these days have a single objective: bowling. That is: keep moving, reaching targets and objectives, increasing the return on investment and pleasing shareholders, whatever it takes, whether their people do so bowling alone or in a league. Don't get me wrong, for many this is what companies are for. But it is precisely this 'bowling, regardless' - whether alone, in groups, in teams or otherwise - that should worry leaders who are interested in the building of social capital.

If Putman is right and his findings could be extrapolated to the nine-to-five world, then, companies that truly profess a 'bowling regardless' philosophy should be in trouble in the long run. They risk losing the precious wealth of 'associability', the voluntary association of individuals in order to obtain a collective gain above the individual gain. A corporation of loners would be the equivalent of Putman's 'nation of loners' and it would be equally dangerous because of its false appearance of 'league-bowling'. As leader-builder you need to decide what kind of bowling you want!

The third component of the organization's I.Q. assets is architectural capital. This has to do with 'ways of doing' and 'ways of being organized'. I will explore some of these aspects in the face 'How you do it'.

The leader-builder-architect creates environments where collective I.Q. grows. He is a leader of tangible and intangible assets and the houses he built can be seen as his legacy.

Legacy

A leader can certainly be judged by his legacy. I usually ask people in my seminars to describe how they would prefer to be remembered as leaders. I do that as part of something broader that I call 'The Pub Test' (living in England, I simply must refer to this pillar of social intercourse.) Ten years from now there is a reunion of this leadership team. Most of them left the organization a while ago. What would be the language, the theme of conver-sation and the description of what was left behind? Here is a typical output example of this exercise:

What you build

The 2016 Reunion – Pub Test

The company itself
There were 'opportunities'…
Learning experience
Innovation, chance to influence
Progressive environment

Our divisions, our own teams
Winning attitudes
High expectations, high rewards
Opportunities for people's
development
Influencing corporate
Risk taking
Source of knowledge to our
customers
Cross-functionality as way of
life

We as management team
Action and decisions
Influencing beyond our own
R&D function
Flexible, driving on change
Diversity paid off
Acknowledged stretch
Great opportunities for personal
and professional development

Me/You
Energetic
Stimulating
Committed
Challenging
Trying
Achiever
Flexible
'changed something'
Created a work environment

It doesn't have to be a very sophisticated output, but when you start asking people about legacy and questions about 'ten years from now', what starts as a light exercise usually ends up giving a solid view of the current values and beliefs. It definitely says a lot about (the visions of leadership in) a particular group. Indeed, the 'proof' of the values is the legacy. The legacy becomes *the* inexcusable window to what leadership was about.

You can lead an organization and leave behind an increase in market share of 4.5% and a P/E ratio the joy of stock analysts. You can lead an organization and leave behind a great behavioural fabric that attracts talent. You can lead an organization and leave behind significant collective eldership capabilities. You can also lead an organization and leave behind the shade of your ego as big as a cathedral. You can leave nothing. You can lead misery. You can lead joy. Or combinations thereof!

► Legacy traps

The best legacy is always a beyond-me leadership. A great period led by a leader followed by the absence of new leaders tells you a lot about the leader's view of himself. Succession is as important as tenure. Great tenures followed by bad successions always make me very suspicious of the greatness of the tenure.

For many years, Max De Pree was the CEO of Herman Miller, a pioneering furniture company that, at times, went through difficult periods. During those, De Pree led firmly with a mixture of deeply rooted Christian values, extraordinary personal commitment and closeness to every employee, and a professed 'servant ethos'. It paid off. Loyalty was very high, both in bad times and better times.
I am told that he was deeply involved in the finding of his successor. You would have thought that whoever went to sit on De Pree's chair (and the company creators of the Aeron chair know a thing or two about sitting!) would have exhibited similar values and behaviours. The reality was that

the first post-De Pree CEO was fired by the Herman Miller family and the second in command resigned. Although I don't claim to know the whole story, there was something there about an incredible legacy-fiasco that makes you think about the mechanisms that some leaders use to establish their own succession. I always draw people's attention to a De Pree syndrome!

There is also a form of prostituted legacy that is very toxic. It happens when the leader projects himself above the judgement of the current organization (followers), dismissing that judgement as less relevant than the one that 'history' will provide. The 'history-will-judge-me' type of leader exhibits a great deal of arrogance by assuming that his greatness can only be understood by people in the distance. This assumption of man-or-woman-of-history, a history-maker, de facto closes the doors to a rational scrutiny today. Many political leaders see themselves in that way; some clearly articulate it, like British Prime Minister, Tony Blair. At least this has the benefit of honesty with the consequent transparency of the dimensions of the ego.

Questions

Time, space, homes, legacy: these are the components to consider as leader-architect. This is my suggested list, but it will never be complete until you add your own questions.

- Use the list to trigger new questions or to attempt to answer them! Make notes, use the book!
- Commit to one single step to 'answer the question'. These steps may look like actions you want to take, questions you want to ask other people in your organization or 'practice' that you want to do at your next opportunity.

Time/ Space

- Do I protect my own time? Do I protect time for others?
- Is my calendar in charge of me? Do I control my appointments?
- Am I, with my leadership style, triggering a culture of no-time-no-space?
- Am I an 'I/we don't have time' person or an 'I/we have plenty of time' person? Does it matter?
- What am I projecting to others?
- Am I leading a 'fast', a 'fast track', a 'speed' and/or an 'urgency' organization? Could I/we explore the differences between these? What are the pros and the liabilities of them?
- Is my leadership one of 'doing all the time' and 'no time for being'?
- How am I fostering a sense of belonging in people?

- Do I create space for people? Am I aware of the needs of 'space' in my organization? Of the types of space that my people want? Have I asked?
- Am I creating or building 'walls' for my people, for the organization? Am I a builder? Yes, but of 'walls'?
- Am I aware of my own 'walls'? Am I in control? Do I hear the builders?

Homes

- How do I foster Human Capital?
- Does my leadership create hubs for talent? Do we have an external war? Do we know how we host talent in our organization?
- Do I treat people as 'investors', or as cost, or as 'valuable assets'?
- Am I a good talent-pool investment-fund-manager?
- Do I foster internal collaborations? Do I do so beyond teams? Do I 'allow' looser networks of connections?
- Am I a leader promoting or fostering associability?
- Do I care about the 'bowling'? Are we bowling together? Bowling regardless?
- How do I tolerate, cope with or perhaps nurture the ambiguity needed to host collaboration by design (teams) AND emerging, spontaneous collaborations (networks)?
- How comfortable do I feel about leading that 'less visible organization' of networks of connections inside?
- What kind of leader am I to a web of external collaborations?
- Do I see collaboration as a key competence, as in "collaboration-R-us"?

Legacy

- What would be my Pub Test results?
- Do I know/have I thought about my legacy, what I would be remembered for?
- What kind of language would people use to describe my leadership capacity in terms of 'houses'?
- What am I leaving behind?
- What are we all leaving behind?
- Do I care about my short-term visible legacy?

ACTION MAP
(some first pass questions)

Me   **My organization**

Me

Questions:
Do I see myself as a builder, as an architect?

Questions:
What am I leaving behind ?

My organization

Questions:
Would people around me see me as leader creating 'spaces' for them?

Questions:
What kind of organization are we building collectively? What are we hosts of?

This is a very simple set of questions to get you started with your reflections and actions. Use the blank pages to record your own questions and notes

▶ *Your Questions and Notes:*

What you build

▶ *Your Questions and Notes:*

The Leader with Seven Faces

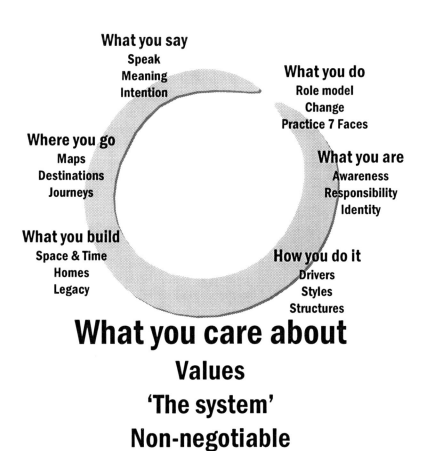

What you say
Speak
Meaning
Intention

What you do
Role model
Change
Practice 7 Faces

Where you go
Maps
Destinations
Journeys

What you are
Awareness
Responsibility
Identity

What you build
Space & Time
Homes
Legacy

How you do it
Drivers
Styles
Structures

What you care about
Values
'The system'
Non-negotiable

4

What you care about

Values
'The system'
Non-negotiable

"How do we decide what is of lasting value in ourselves in a society which is impatient, which focuses on the immediate moment?"
Richard Sennett[14]

Every time I have been confronted with the question, "Define value, please?", I have never found a better answer than, *"What you care about"*. I know that it sounds a bit broad... but *"What is it that you care about?"* is the best possible question to ask in order to understand a value system, whether explicit or hidden. This face of the leader is about the foundations of values and beliefs behind everything else, the anchors to 'systems' - whether personal or organizational - that trigger many of our behaviours. Leaders who are strong in this area present a face that focuses strongly on the

---

[14] Sennett, Richard, 1998, *The corrosion of character: Personal consequences of work in the new capitalism*, W.W. Norton & Company Inc., New York

language (and hopefully behaviours) of beliefs. It is as if precisely this 'what-one-cares-about' defines all activities and the rest of the thinking. I'd like to bring three themes here for our conversation:

- **Values:** those drivers with the capacity to 'explain' almost everything else: what we do, what we say and perhaps the image we project onto the external world.

- **'The system':** How we tend to attribute power and control to a vaguely amalgamated concept of processes and rules in the organization which often we use as 'value system above us'. It sometimes represents a great and effective way to relinquish personal responsibility: it is the culture, it is not me, it's the system, sorry! In 'the system', leaders sometimes find the alibi for their behaviours. What a marvellous smokescreen!

- **What's non-negotiable:** perhaps by defining what can and can't be changed, puts us in a better position to defend what we truly believe is core to us and to the organization.

Values

There is a vast amount of literature about values and beliefs and I am not going to pretend that we could summarize it here. As in any other dimension that we are (jointly) exploring in this book, I am more interested in pointing at directions for questions (good questions, uncomfortable questions) than in having yet another system, framework or classification to glorify or to follow. I am also more interested in simple observations that could help us with those questions. For example, the ones that follow…

1. Declared values and real values are not necessarily the same. Many corporations these days have a declared set of values. But it doesn't mean that those are alive. In many cases, the day-to-day behaviours of managers and leaders in that organization may be in total contradiction with the set of declared values.

2. 'Value' shares with 'behaviour' the enormous potential of being interpreted on demand. These words represent semantic moving targets. Using the language does not necessarily mean that the day-to-day life is lived under the supposed reality behind the language.

3. Take a standard list, like the following one:

Achievement (sense of)	Excellence	Leadership	Relationships
Adventure	Excitement	Love, being loved	Religion, religiosity
Altruism	Fairness	Loyalty	Reputation
Caring	Fame	Market position	Responsibility
Challenging problems	Fast living	Meaningful work	Security
Change and variety	Financial gain	Merit	Self-respect
Close relationships	Financial security	Money	Serenity
Community (sense of)	Freedom	Nature	Sincerity
Competence	Friendships	Order	Sophistication
Competition	Growth	Personal development	Stability
Cooperation	Having a family	Physical challenge	Time freedom
Creativity	Helping other people	Pleasure	Transparency
Credibility	Helping society	Power and authority	Trust
Decisiveness	Innovation	Privacy	Truth
Democracy	Integrity	Promotion	Wealth
Ecological awareness	Intellectual status	Public service	Wisdom
Effectiveness	Involvement	Purity	Work
Efficiency	Job fulfilment	Quality (total)	
Ethical practice	Knowledge	Recognition, status	

This list is a compilation of several sources where the concept mentioned has been used as 'value'. You have here a combination of many things. Some of these values fall into the category of what has been called 'end-status values' - that is, situations or states that are worth achieving. Other concepts are more 'means-values' or ways of doing (behaving, living, managing, leading). Very often there is a fine line between the two categories. The list, if anything, is one of desires, aspirations. Good. I'm sure you would agree that you and I may need to have a conversation about what we mean by many, if not all, of these things.

The language of values is not terribly operational but its popularity comes from its utility: it provides a good fabric for conversation! As a leader, don't use it unless you are prepared to explain, define, articulate and translate the meaning behind it. To say, for example, that 'we value honesty because it generates trust' is a reasonable statement in itself. It is so reasonable, that you and I may run the risk of assuming that we share the meaning of the words. And we may fool ourselves. Bypassing the 'checking', may lead to actions that could go in different directions, behaviours that look inconsistent with the values!

4. Values can conflict with each other. One of the most well-expressed and thought-provoking ideas of conflict of this kind has been articulated by Richard Sennett - Professor of Sociology at both the London School of Economics and MIT - in his little book *The corrosion of character* (W.W. Norton & Company Inc., 1998). The concept is simple. Business life these days takes us to a rather short-term,

short-lived, fast, ephemeral 'way of life', short-term expectations and short-term cycles. There is no 'career for life' anymore, many organizations appear and disappear quickly. 'Flexibility' (of jobs, personal security, skills and competences) has become a value per se, often an unquestionable mantra. Challenging this would lead you to find yourself on a list of the politically - or managerially! - incorrect. On the other hand, individuals living and working in that context, usually have longer term aims and goals for themselves, their families, their children etc. One hardly wants to install ephemeral values in one's children! This contradiction between the two worlds, leads - according to Sennett - to what he calls a 'corrosion of the character'. I personally believe that one of the duties of the leader is to spot those potential conflicts, those 'double binds', those contradictory values, and assess the consequences. It may not always end up in a clear answer, but at least the awareness may go a long way towards dealing with it.

5. We are living in times of pseudo-meta-values. Pardon my language! I mean the abuse of 'super-value language' with the goal of providing an overall, blank justification for our actions as individuals and leaders. There have always been those pseudo-meta-values, as I call them, in the religious, social and political arena. But today, we have a few of them pretending to have the power to make most other values totally secondary and dependent, if not irrelevant. My prototype is the new Holy Trinity of integrity, sincerity and honesty. Leaders who profess total honesty, often use that declaration as a justification for other things. The same applies to integrity and sincerity. Many years ago, I spotted an American cartoon where one of the

characters said: "*If I am so honest, how can I be wrong?*" It may make you smile, but don't take it lightly. Many leaders today seem to be judged almost only on the basis of their sincerity and honesty. We even have the language for it: "*At least you can't say he is not honest, or he is not sincere, etc.*" as if that was an overriding justification for everything else.

But you could say that this Holy Trinity of values is nothing more than a baseline, a given. One expects honesty, sincerity and integrity from leaders, but those do not constitute a vaccination against error, misjudgements or other 'corrosions'. British Prime Minister, Tony Blair, is a master of referring to the Holy Trinity of values as a justification for his political behaviour. I still haven't heard many people challenging the supposedly overriding power of those values. I would say to the Blair-like-leaders: "*You may be sincere and honest, but you may be totally wrong. Or you may not. Besides, your personal sincerity and integrity is simply a pass for you to hold office, and it is otherwise irrelevant for any further socio-political discourse.*" Translation: "*We take your sincerity-honesty for granted. Now, can we talk about the things we should be talking about?*" A similar use of a supposed super-value is the appeal to or recognition of 'consistency'. 'He is a very consistent leader' people may say. It is said as if consistency inevitably leads to the Holy Trinity. And, as the cartoon says, if you are so consistent (on top of honest, integral and sincere), surely you must also be right! Just one small observation: Hitler was very consistent.

6. There are living values and dead values. By that, I do not mean negative values or values leading to death, but values that have been declared and even articulated but whose life stopped at that point. The opposite (living values) means that there is a mechanism in the system (the organization, the leadership team) to continuously check for the reality of the stated value. Any value could be a living or a dead one; the concept of the value per se does not predict it. Let's take innovation, for example. This is one very commonly stated in companies today. If we declare innovation as a value, then surely we should have a mechanism in place to find out if we innovate or not. It is not necessarily product innovation that I am talking about. It is idea innovation, ways of doing innovation, new solutions innovation, etc. Imagine that you have a crisis and solve it fast and properly. If you really care about innovation, you should ask yourself, "*Have my team and I dealt with this as we always do? Or have we looked at new ways or alternatives in our dealing with the problem?*" If the answer is, "*No, we never do, we have good processes and we keep on repeating them*", well, good news for the efficiency of the system but there is no innovation-life in that piece of managerial response. The concept of values sort-of-implies that you should stick to them! But if you don't check them - or even if there is no provision in the organization for checking them - then they belong to the museum of Good Ideas and Even Better Intentions.

Sennett told us about the corrosion of our character in rather personal terms. It is 'my character' versus 'the organization'. But there are also other forms of corrosion beyond what Sennett describes. It has to do with us avoiding any uncomfortable value conflict by attributing the power of decision and action outside ourselves. And we have invented a marvellous mechanism: the system.

'The System'

This is a true story. Not many people knew what was going on in the Psychology department. Nothing unusual about that. Campus activities did not always hit headlines. The advert in the local newspaper was good enough to attract volunteers. A few dollars for participating in an experiment on 'learning'. Many people from the city of New Haven applied. It was easy money of the kind offered from time to time for one-off 'jobs' at the university. What people didn't know - and didn't need to know - is that this time it was a repetition of social experiments already held with students. University students have always been the primary source for any 'volunteer study'. Handy extra money for doing this and that in several departments. Psychology was one of them. But now the participants were normal citizens from the town. Professor Milgram wondered if the findings would be similar.

Stanley Milgram was a small man, a curious assistant professor with an ability to design social experiments of all sorts. This time the town volunteers, as the students before, were asked to be part of a test to study how punishment - as administered by some sort of electric shock - had an effect on learning. The instructed volunteer conducting the experiment ('teacher') read sequences of words to another person ('learner') who needed to repeat them: house, money, flower, pretty, whether, cat. Each time the 'learner' got it wrong, the volunteer-teacher from New Haven administered a small electric shock from the other side of the window in the adjacent room. They didn't see each other but had met before the experiment begun.

The administrator-teacher could see the reaction of the subject who was sitting on a sort of 'electric chair'. The administrator was also asked by the psychologist instructor to progressively increase the potency of the shock with each mistake made by the 'learner' subject. It could be done by moving up the lever: 25V, 30V, 40V, etc. Obviously, the reaction of the subject in the other room went from an unpleasant face at first, to a more and more uncomfortable feeling. If the subject kept making mistakes, the psychologist would instruct the administrator to increase the potency. Invariably, it got to very unpleasant, even unbearable. More mistakes, more volts. The subject was almost screaming. "*Never mind*", the psychologist said, "*this is a well-controlled experiment, you need to keep pushing the button.*" Screams. "*I want to stop, he wants to get out*", many people on the 'teacher' side said. "*No, keep trying, it's the protocol, we can't break this experiment yet*", said the psychologist. All that continued until people were literally shaking in the other room. But the administrators kept pushing the button under the instructors' instructions. Well, some of them. 65% to be precise. The other 35% gave up and refused to continue the torture.

The experiments were repeated and repeated, always the same: mistakes, shocks, up, up, up, and the citizen from New Haven - as the university student did before - pushing the button despite the guy on the other side of the screen being tortured. But the experiments were for the common good, to study the effects of punishment on learning, a noble aim.

Again and again 65 % complied with instructions, 35 % told the psychologist to get a life and keep the money. More screams, more shocks and more knowledge about learning. The reality: 65% percent of normal citizens from the pretty normal town of New Haven were prepared to administer increasingly potent shocks to increasingly terrified fellow human beings, for a few bucks, for science and following instructions. But there was a small trick. Nobody really got shocked, the fellows on the other side were always actors pretending to get near to convulsion each time the normal citizen pushed the button.

These experiments were known exclusively in the academic field for a long time and they also suffered the normal academic scrutiny. To this day, they are still controversial. Officially labelled 'obedience' experiments, some academic psychologists argued that it wasn't obedience they measured, but trust. Other discussions were (and are) about their true social meaning. Could we extrapolate those laboratory findings to real life? Regarding this, tons of pages were written: half in favour, half against. For many, these were a sort of 'post-holocaust' (which is when the experiments were done) soul-searching attempt to understand how normal human beings could be drawn to obey orders.

Other groups of social psychologists have focused the attention on what could distinguish the 65% from the other 35%. Is there a particular 'personality' that correlates with one or the other? Could we predict who would keep pushing the button? To this day, there are no good answers to any of these questions and we are left with the hard facts: 65 % of us (I know, I know, not you) will keep on obeying the instructions.

▶ *It's the system, not me*

For people alien to the behavioural sciences, this is pretty unexpected, surprising and possibly disturbing news. My many years as a practicing psychiatrist have made me slightly cynical about human nature and I am not half as disturbed as probably many of you. I have been spectator to many kinds of human misery not in the public domain. But 'the Milgram experiments' are a bit distinctive. They are not dealing with psychiatrically disturbed individuals or even psychologically unfit people. These were normal students and normal citizens who pulled the trigger. No matter how many tons of academic papers refine the data, criticize the methodology, pontificate about the 'social transfer principle' (whether laboratory experiments' findings can be extrapolated) or argue whether it's obedience, trust, authority or hidden sadism being measured, one can't get away from the fact that these real people inflicted what they thought was real pain to fellow people, just by following orders.

The good news is, in the leadership world, we don't have electric shocks, so we don't have to worry about this. The bad news is that there are worse things than an electric shock to inflict pain. It's called psychological pain. In our organizations, the dynamics of power are very rich. We exercise power, obey orders, follow instructions. We also challenge them, resist them or decide not to comply. In the process, organizational life sometimes serves as the big umbrella context and excuse for many things - that would not be accepted in 'normal life' – to be accepted under the power of 'the system', 'the way we do things', 'the management team', 'the board', 'the process', 'the culture', 'the SOP', etc. How many times have we said, or heard: "*It's not me, it's the system. If it were me, I would let you do/have x,y,z, but I have to follow the instructions. This is what they ask me to do".*

I have always been fascinated by the pervasive use of 'they' in organizations. 'They' want this or that, 'they' force me to do that, 'they' want it that way. What has fascinated me even more is not the times when 'they' is used by junior people - which one could understand as referring to the powerful upper management - but how often I have heard it used by very senior people almost at the top, if not the top itself. I have wondered, who is 'they' in those cases? Certainly, in my experience, it's a sort of virtual 'they', an invisible 'they', an almost Olympic 'they' that justifies many things. 'They' is 'the system' and 'the system' is the best possible and most convenient, highly unaccountable, management black hole.

We don't need the man in the white coat in Milgram's lab to tell us, *"Keep pushing, it's an experiment. For goodness sake, do you think you can break the protocol just like that?"* Our managers and supervisors and directors and vice-presidents, you and me - or perhaps 65% of us, if Milgram is right - will say, *"I am sorry, John, it's not me, it's the system. I have to inflict this pain on you. I don't really want to do that, but I have no choice. They want me to do it."*

It comes in many forms and shapes. Here are some examples:

- o 30 volts: forcing people to do things that are a hassle, unnecessary, and serve no purpose other than ego boosting to the one who gives the instructions, under the: *"It's not me, it's the SOP"*.

o 50 volts: denying that little, perhaps one-off, flexible time that would make all the difference to the employee's family and no difference whatsoever to the business, under the: "*It's not me. If it were me, you could have it, but I need to follow the procedure*".

o Higher voltage: submitting somebody to unnecessary humiliation and considerable psychological pain by requesting an action that serves no purpose other than public show of power and control over the individual. I have seen the latter done to somebody at a time where the employee was going through a terrible family crisis. Nevertheless, she was told: "*I am sorry, we have to do this, it's the system. Sorry that it has to be done now, but there is nothing I can do*". It was a fantastic lie; there was a lot the manager could have done.

o Higher voltage: a manager decides to leave the company and hands in his resignation. He is going to a competitor. Suddenly panic explodes in the legal department and in the managing director's office. The resigning manager is escorted outside the building with no time to explain to his staff, treated like a mixture of terrorist and industrial spy, and for hours humiliated personally and socially under 'the system', 'the procedure' or 'they want us to do this'. I have seen it many times, again and again. The practice is both pure voltage application and highly stupid. It assumes, amongst other things, that it's something really useful to 'security' by preventing the manager to, what? Steal the content of his filing cabinet? Make a copy of his hard disc? Since it insults the intelligence of the resigning manager (who has had plenty of time to copy the entire company computer if he wanted to), it serves no real business purpose and it's highly humiliating and painful. The only conclusion is that both the entire legal department and the entire office of the managing director are populated by stupid people. Or – and this is even more scary - that they are otherwise rather normal 'citizens-of-New-Haven' who follow (stupid) orders from 'the system'.

How each of us manages the different 'psychological voltage' is rather personal. A low voltage for me may be a high voltage for you. But all of us, I bet, have cases of: "*It's not me, it's the system. Here you go, a little shock (or a big shock). I know you are going to scream, but there is little I can do. It's the system. If it were me, I wouldn't do it.*" The most worrying thing of all is that *we* are all citizens of New Haven, not personality disorders waiting for the opportunity to strike. OK, there are some exceptions.

One of the mechanisms that 'the system' has to exercise its power is the distribution of the script between the characters: the legal department, the HR department, the office of the CEO. There is plenty of script to play with in organizational life, plenty of characters, plenty of plots. Let's look at more psychosocial experiments!

▶ Roles, power and uniforms

The pictures that shocked the world will still be in many people's minds when Abu Ghraib, the name of the place, will be forgotten. Iraqi prisoners reduced to humiliating displaying flesh. American custodians laughing, harassing, abusing or passing by in the corridor. All these scenes on the front page and primetime everywhere. With the exception of universal disgust, the spectrum of reactions varied amongst people. There were - and still are - the politico-military questions: *"How on earth could this happen? Were they just a few bad apples? How far up in the chain of command?"* There was - and still is - the socio-political question: "H*ow much abuse, torture and the fine line between them can be justified, was justified or is justified?"* And there was - and still is - the plain, normal citizen question: "H*ow on earth can a human being do this to others?"* Blame was scattered in several directions, but the buck has stopped somewhere, or so we are told. And the whole thing will soon be more or less diluted into history. The American writer, Gore Vidal, reacted to the 9/11 New York events with a sharp, cynical and otherwise politically incorrect comment: *"It will all be over by the Christmas sales"*. It didn't quite happen like that, as we know, but he wanted to make the point of how fragile our collective memory is. The Abu Ghraib saga, I suspect, will be contained one way or another, but will soon be consigned to a black book of black history, period.

Amongst the thousands of articles and references to the events, an unpretentious, not terribly prominent and very much matter-of-fact column in *The New York Times* revealed that - at least for a tiny sector of the population - these events were no surprise whatsoever. Anybody who has ever taken a serious degree in Social Psychology would have reacted with: *"Aha! Here we go again. Milgram and Zimbardo revisited"*.

I referred to Stanley Milgram above. In the Zimbardo experiments, a prison was totally recreated in the basement of

Stanford University with a proper set of cells, offices, corridors, lights and other paraphernalia. A group of students was invited to participate in the study of role playing and execution. The group was split into two. One group would play guards and the other detainees. The whole thing was about recreating real life in jail. The game started with adequate role playing, with full use of appropriate gear for the guards and the detainees. Both parts took it seriously, as you would expect from loyal students committed to the experiment. Whilst 'the guards' gave orders and more orders, shouted more and more and reached abuse, the detainees on the receiving end were submitted to all of the above and 'typical jail punishments', such as workouts.

The roles were lived intensively, the atmosphere became progressively tense, some of the 'detainees' protested, *"Hey, guys, come on. This is just a game, an experiment, time out!"* But the guards reacted stronger and stronger. More workouts, more punishment. Fiction became reality and reality was very hard. It was so hard that the experiment had to be stopped well before it was due to finish, because somebody was going to get killed and many seriously wounded!

Social Psychology studies topics such as these, often labelled as issues of obedience, conformity, authority, attribution, etc. Just for the record, as in the example of the Milgram experiments described above, we are not talking here about psychopaths or deviant personalities, but normal students and volunteers. And as I said before, this is precisely the scary part. In theory, any of us could behave in the same way.

In Social Psychology courses, the lecturer invariably asks the class to guess the results before he explains them. Invariably, classes are optimistic and always wrongly predict a very low number of who would 'obey' or 'conform'. Also regularly the students are asked afterwards whether they could do the same in similar circumstances and, guess what? Consistently they say, "*Not me*"..

So, give people roles (and titles) and uniforms (cloth or mental ones) and be ready for the unpredictable. 'Roles' and 'uniforms' allow us to exercise power in a legitimized way, under a given authority (be that the boss, the chain of command or 'the system'). Like the Stanford students of Zimbardo, or the normal citizens of New Haven of Milgram, we may even take it very seriously.

'Roles and uniforms' are powerful creators of new personae. Once we get them, we are ready for a daily Greek tragedy and a chameleonic transformation into a caring manager, a despot, a Samaritan, a sadist, 'a teacher', 'a learner', a dictator, a leader, a ruthless Prince, a benign King, a foot soldier, a general, a preacher, a follower, an administrator of electric or psychological shocks, a tutor, a mentor, a smiling Buddhist monk or an arms dealer. If anything, Social Sciences teaches us about our incredibly plastic capacity which we are always more ready to attribute to others - particular deviant people - than to ourselves.

And this fantastic capacity is precisely the good news-bad news to consider. Bad news à la Iraq. Good news for the possibly good potential that 'roles and uniforms' provide us on the daily life stage. That is, when leadership is exercised for the common good! And since most of our daily life is spent at work, all the above applies to daily life in management and leadership of organizations.

Another newspaper article that I read at the time of the Iraq prison disclosure was cynical about the 'new' Iraqi police. The occupying forces had finally realized that there was no other option but to bring back the old police and the old military that - in the greatest naiveté of all - they had disbanded without any alternative before. The columnist made some jokes about 'seeing the old moustaches and the old faces back' and seemed desperate to understand how on earth we could expect a new behaviour and 'conversion' from them overnight. Again, most people would be sympathetic with this question, whilst that tiny minority - belonging to the Social Psychology tribe - would have no problem in accepting that this is indeed possible.

If the context changes (and it had indeed in those situations) this 'new Police' would surprise people with its ability to 'submit' and 'comply' with the new regime. Social Sciences are telling us: "*It doesn't have to be bad news*". A change of uniform (even in the literary sense!) and new role context may create 'good', even for the old moustaches.

Similarly, providing a right positive context in daily life in organizations (the role of the leaders) makes roles and uniforms constructive. The same roles and uniforms (managers, directors, project leaders, Heads of HR, vice-presidents….) in a negative context create havoc. The key is the existence or absence of an overall agreement on 'non-negotiable behaviours', hopefully linked to a value system. These non-negotiable behaviours were probably absent in Abu Ghraib, to say the least. Or otherwise, everything there was possible and negotiable in a contingent way ('depending on what we need to achieve', for example).

▶ *It depends*

Contingent approaches in management and leadership are wonderfully convenient and deeply dangerous, not something that traditional business education is prepared to accept. My unofficial father of 'contingent leadership' is Jack Welch, ex-CEO of GE, who could go from nasty to caring (admittedly mostly the former) 'depending on what was needed', as he himself confessed more than once. My bias in our own leadership approach through the work we do with organizations is that one of the most dangerous management statements of all is 'it depends', but you may think that I am too radical. After all, what's wrong with adapting to situations and behaving 'depending on the objectives'?

Milgram, Zimbardo and my own old clinical psychiatry work have taught me a long time ago that it's precisely our own plastic capacity that - when married to the 'it depends' - generates a recipe for disaster. That's why I prefer solid non-negotiable rules of the game in management - even if I may disagree with them - to loose, relativist, contingent, 'it depends' leadership that scares me more than Milgram's fake shock machines. The problem is not in the moustaches, but in what the moustaches are allowed to do when they play guards or detainees, teachers or learners, leaders or followers.

▶ *Social responsibility begins at home*

Talk to anybody about social responsibility of a company and the first images that come to mind are the rain forest in Brazil and the need for its preservation, the need for conservation and for a stop to pollution of the environment. Then come the images of the abomination of the sweatshops in the Far East where small children are manufacturing T-shirts for the West. In other words, things far away from home, big multinational stuff and sins of globalization that the street warriors fight by burning McDonalds' franchises.

'Society' and 'social responsibility' are nice concepts that - even if a bit vague, a bit idealistic and a bit moralistic - fit very well in mission statements. After all, imagine the alternative. Do you know of any company that may want to declare they wish to pollute, destroy or run concentration camps?

The trouble with far-away so-called social responsibility is that it distracts from what is happening next door or downstairs. Companies that are 'socially responsible' - by the stereotype standards of no-pollution-no-child-labour - may, in fact, be running socially irresponsible policies internally with their own staff. Sumantra Ghoshal, the late professor of the London Business School, liked to refer to the atmosphere of some companies as 'Calcutta in summer', a suffocating environment, not measured in centigrade or Fahrenheit. Some of those companies may have mission statements referring to commitments of social responsibility that prevent them from polluting rivers, but they may ignore the daily pollution of the minds of the work force.

Let's face it, Ghoshal was right. Some working environments are not nice! High levels of internal politics and personal wars, disregard for the life of employees who are numbers on a spreadsheet, and irrational 'contingency policies' (hire fast/fire fast) may lead to a 'Calcutta in summer' workplace, even if the company swears never to dump a chemical in the nearby river.

▶ *Rain forests at home*

Social responsibility, like charity, begins at home, in the manager's office next door and downstairs in the HR department and the labs. It has to do with understanding that people spend a great deal of their daily life working for organizations of some sort and that the company - whether it wants to recognize it or not - has a 'social responsibility' for them. A responsibility that involves a duty to provide an environment that respects the individual, enhances the human condition and values the employee. Surely, if it's good for trees, it must be good for humans. Those who think this is airy-fairy stuff are no different from those who think that the pollution of the river by the chemical plant is a necessary evil, unavoidable if business is to meet its objectives. Years ago, such people got away with murder because the population was either largely ignorant of the issue, silent or insensitive. Today, such practices make headlines that backfire on the company in a way that it can't afford. Probably, some years from now, the Calcutta-in-summer workplaces will make headlines in a similar way, with similar consequences. But not yet.

One of the behaviours one finds in socially-less-than-responsible environments is a frequent schizophrenia of the leader's mind. Outside the office, a leader may be a (sort of) kind, civilized and perhaps church-going human being. In the office, he may transform himself into a careless nine-to-five leader who, quite frankly, may not give a damn about the 'environment' as long as 'the numbers are achieved' (and his bonus is safe). Perfectly reasonable human beings become very unreasonable managers overnight as if affected by some sort of toxic gas on leaving the company's car park and entering the office. Once in the office, toxic management takes over. It's as circadian as night and day.

▶ Perfect abdications

The company's obvious need to have policies and procedures is a perfect excuse for the toxicity that leads to Calcutta-summer-like environments. I have mentioned above the "*Sorry, it's not me, I have to do this, it's company policy*", the "*If it were up to me, I would allow this, but I don't make the rules*", the "*I can't allow you to do that, as then everybody will expect the same*", etc. The interesting thing is that many mangers who hide behind 'company policies' and 'I don't make the rules' or 'I have to treat everyone the same way' are simply lying: in many cases, they have the power and ability to interpret company policy using their own brain, to grant an exception to the rule and to accord the individual case with a special concession because common sense tells him that the rule was not invented to make life difficult or to intoxicate the environment of the workplace.

One of the best defence systems that toxic leadership of the Calcutta-Summer type has is the one that uses 'internal equity' as an all-seasons argument. "*We must see the equity aspects of this issue in the organization,*" a manager or an HR leader will say, "*We can't give this to Smith or it will set a precedent for others*". That kind of argument assumes many things, but one that has always puzzled me is that it assumes that the entire organization may want the same as Smith. In practical terms, this is not true in most cases. Take an example that I know very well from my own experience. I did an MBA sponsored by my employer at that time. There were no rigid criteria that I remember about who could do it. I knew a couple of colleagues like myself who were sponsored. My boss did not have a long queue of people in his office wanting to do an MBA! As a matter of fact, it was hard work that some of us did on top of our normal workload. But in many other organizations, such a thing could never have existed because (here it comes): "*It would not have been fair in terms of internal equity*!" Since then, I have repeated this positive behaviour myself when I was in a greater position of 'power'. A few of my direct and indirect reports got sponsored for a distance learning MBA. The pattern was the same. I didn't have a queue of requests at my door because, as in my case, I was sponsoring long evenings at the computer whilst keeping up with daily responsibilities. Despite that, the HR old guard didn't like it!

▶ *Fairness, the greatest parapet*

Another toxic word that can be used both *ad libitum* and with a great deal of semantic discretion: fairness. Many managers – and many HR departments – are great defenders of fairness and seem obsessed with it. And yet, under this parapet, they may exhibit the greatest unfair behaviour of all: the unfairness of homogenization. Fairness, as unilaterally dictated and interpreted, may boost the moral ego of the manager but may not go far with anybody else. Extraordinary salary differences between the top and the bottom, executive privileges, Boards driven by personal gain, etc. are not fair, yet they are part of daily life, often in the same company, where the HR department is fighting for trivial 'differences in fairness' about, for example, minor increases in salaries at the bottom end of the salary scales.

Organizational and business life may be a highly rewarding and enlightening human activity. And, yes, work also takes place in non-Calcutta-summer places. Leaders and leaders-to-be need to uncover any possible corporate cynicism about so-called social responsibility, where people are really talking about a good track record of clean rivers, but having a work environment that at best is not worth working in and toxic at worst.

When mental pollution internally replaces external pollution, the company is socially irresponsible, despite all their 'care for the environment'. Let me get personal here! I can't stand those perfect environmentalists 'who care' about recycling the memos, who bin all the metal cans in special containers and use the same hotel towel every day so they don't squander water, but who - at the same time - pollute the environment of their own teams and people working for them.

▶ Pending revolutions

The customer revolution took place in the 80s with a proliferation of customer services departments as an innovation. Today, these are the baseline; they don't even inspire admiration anymore. You're supposed to have them. Other revolutions of the past are the bread and butter of today. The Quality movement focused on quality as a final end. Today, this is the baseline, the entry pass. In a few years' time, you won't see an ISO logo in letterheads or on the company van.

The shareholder revolution is incipient in some quarters; boards and management are being more and more scrutinized in their actions (and levels of rewards). I don't think we have seen anything big yet. The ever-pending revolution is the employee revolution. At that point, toxic leadership will be uncovered and companies that are socially irresponsible internally will make headlines. Those companies that are brave enough to look at themselves in the mirror and identify those socially irresponsible internal practices, and who are then also brave enough to do something about it, will win the game. Amen.

You and I know companies full of 'nice people'. In many cases, though, it's as if we were saying: "*Individually, we're all basically good guys. Collectively, however, we can be a bunch of arrogant people who use the excuse of rules dictated by somewhere else to exercise power and control*". If a working environment has the ability to produce or nurture Calcutta-in-summer-like leaders who are otherwise 'nice guys individually', this environment is toxic. You live in a polluted environment, and should avoid it if you can. And that's the problem: the 'if you can'. After all, a few million people live in Calcutta. Many can't afford to be anywhere else and, indeed, some may even like summer there or be unable to imagine anything better.

Social responsibility is not a green issue or an ethical corporate governance approach with the idea of not polluting rivers and not cutting trees in Brazil. These are all well and good. But social responsibility must begin at home. That is, in the office next door, the manufacturing plant or the project team, not that you'll find this on a business school curriculum.

Non-negotiable

When Collins and Porras did their research on organizations that seemed to have been 'built to last'[15], they discovered that one of their commonalities was the existence of and persistence over time of a small set of core values, no matter how much strategic and tactical redirection the company had undertaken. It seemed as if that core of 'non-negotiable' had acted as the pillars that had kept them alive and well. 'Preserve the core, stimulate progress' was a slogan that followed from the findings and the book.

The Collins-Porras story was very popular for a long time and the book is still selling as a business book blockbuster. As in many success stories, there are consultants and academics that don't have a lot of admiration for the 'built to last' concept. It doesn't help that some of the companies highlighted as model have since slipped down in their market performance. It is Tom Peter's *In search of excellence* (Warner Books, 1982) revisited: many of the companies described as mirrors at the time of the publication eventually disappeared. But many of their original findings are still valid even if they now come with a warning on the box: taking them too seriously may damage your health.

---

[15] Collins, James C., Porras, Jerry I, 2004, *Built to Last: Succesful Habits of Visionary Companies*, Harper Collins

I believe that leaders should obsessively look at what is negotiable and what's not in terms of values, beliefs and behaviours, and help make a collective judgement. In times of change, to know what needs to be changed is as important as to know what does not. Sometimes, there is a fine line. Yes, there are risks and judgements to be made. Welcome to leadership. If the leader takes a too-immovable-value-base approach he may risk missing the change needed or the change opportunity. If, on the other hand, the leader plays a contingent-fundamentalism approach ('absolutely everything is negotiable', 'it depends') there is no way any kind of permanent pillar - whether value principle or behaviour - will be stable.

In my work with leaders and organizations I use the term 'non-negotiable' (or the question 'what's non-negotiable?') a lot, as a way to focus on what the organization, the leadership team or the leader himself cares about. Very often this simple question has simply never been on the table. Many organizations operate in automatic pilot mode with little time, energy or interest in looking at themselves in the mirror and ask that fundamental question: "*What do we care about?*" The questioning of the non-negotiable at value/belief level is always healthy because it forces you to decide! And decisions can sometimes be tough, particularly if the leader wants a bit of everything.

You as leader - or your leadership team and yourself - may have decided that your core value system is, for example, innovation, customer focus, personal enhancements of the employee, built trust and teamwork. I am making this up, but many companies may recognize themselves. It is not until the 'what do I (really) care about' question comes in, that leaders may start to see potential conflicts. What if the customer doesn't want (to pay for) innovation? What if personal enhancement of the employee can't happen at the level expected by the employees? And, more importantly, what is the relative weight of those values? Simply put, what is more important, customer focus or personnel enhancement? Would you put equal dollars or pounds to these? You see, even a good set of 'declared values' can have possible conflict built in. The 'what do I care about?' question helps to go through the specifics and define the real pillars that perhaps you as leader don't want to touch, even in very tough times where 'everything' is up for change.

I am leaving this section deliberately short and open because this is true 'discovery land'. If we could sit back and ask this question with enough time to reflect and look at ourselves in the mirror, we all would be on the path of true leadership. In my leadership programmes, I use the term 'uncovering values' in my sessions with some leadership teams, because that is what it really is. The values are there, somewhere, perhaps hidden. I am not talking about the set of declared values which many of my clients usually have as a corporation. But I'm talking about the ones that are behind the attitudes and behaviours of a given leadership team. It would be very easy to assume that they are the same or that there is even a match.

You need a proper process of 'uncovering' or discovery which I provide by inducing discussions on 'non-business items'! In advance, I send materials to read, coming from a variety of sources and places. In many cases, these are of the type that you don't normally see on business desks. The team is confronted with a mixture of news clips, web pages, articles, chapters from books, single slides and many other 'pieces' in order to discuss them within a certain structure, like these Seven Faces. The point is to 'force' people to talk about day-to-day issues in day-to-day language. I want to bring to the meeting room the language of the corridor, the men's and ladies room, the company cafeteria or the reception chairs around the water cooler. And believe me, doing this is an achievement in itself! Confronted with relatively business-jargon-free discussions on various topics, people are good at that process of 'uncovering'. Not only that, but very often the discussion goes towards 'what is not negotiable' or 'what we need to preserve at all cost' or 'what we don't want at all'. The extremes are always easier than the middle road. But it is this individual - or as in this case, collective - process of discovery and uncovering that provides clarity for what is not negotiable. You can call them values, beliefs or behaviours: although these distinctions matter a lot, it is less relevant at this stage than the opportunity to map your framework.

Values, beliefs, and non-negotiable rules of the game are key leadership ingredients. What leaders care about, expressed in one way or another, defines the universe of the collaboration mechanism in the organization. It is moment-of-truth territory. If you care 'about everything', you care about nothing. If you care about a few things, you'd better stick to them and behave accordingly.

Questions

Values, beliefs, non-negotiable rules: you need to know what you care about and act on that.. This is my suggested list, but it will never be complete until you add your own questions.

- Use the list to trigger new questions or to attempt to answer them! Make notes, use the book!
- Commit to one single step to 'answer the question'. These steps may look like actions you want to take, questions you want to ask other people in your organization or 'practice' that you want to do at your next opportunity.

Values

- In your organization, is there a gap between the declared set of values and how things are done in real life?
- If you have a list of declared values, do they feel more or less homogenous or are some very high level and vague and others more concrete?
- Could you identify some 'corrosions of character' in your organization?
- Is your own leadership responsible for any 'corrosion'?
- Have you ever thought about this issue of conflict between values and character?
- As a leader, how much do you use the 'honesty-sincerity and integrity' argument? Do you use it to justify other things or to escape scrutiny, for example?

- Is your organization one in which the language of the above is very prominent? Do people take it seriously?
- Do you have dead values? That is, values that have been declared with the best of intentions but that have never been properly 'translated'? What is the consequence of all this?
- If you have a value system, how often is this compatible with your value X, Y, Z - for you as leader or your leadership team as a group?

'The system'

- Can you identify yourself or your team with the use of the 'umbrella justification' expressed in terms of 'the system', 'our culture', 'the SOPs', etc?
- How is this used/abused?
- Think of the Milgram experiments. Do they mean anything to you?
- Could you see situations of 'obedience' in your organization that may have followed a similar pattern of 'infliction of pain'?
- How much do you or does your organization use the 'they'? And what does it mean for you?
- What's the role and power of 'uniforms' in your organization?
- Have you thought or reflected about the dynamics of power of your close people?
- How much of a contingent leadership is your style? What are /may be the consequences?
- How much 'fairness' and 'internal equity' is used in your organization?

Non-negotiable

- Is your organization 'built to last'?
- Is your leadership style geared towards that? Does it matter?
- Do you have any set of core, non-negotiable values?
- Would you work on getting them clarified or articulated?
- Could you find incompatible values in your organization?
- If you haven't done it, should you try to articulate for yourself and for others 'the non-negotiable'?
- In the chapter about 'what leaders build', we discussed 'legacy'. Do you clearly now what kind of values and non-negotiable 'ways of doing' or behaviours you would like to be remembered for?

What you care about

ACTION MAP
(some first pass questions)

Me   **My organization**

Me

Questions:
Do I recognize/could
I articulate my own
personal value set?

Questions:
Am I providing a
framework for value-
setting for others? Am I
shaping the collective
agreement of what is
'non-negotiable'?

My organization

Questions:
What do other people
around me or the
organization I lead see of
me regarding my
values?

Questions:
Do we have an
organization where 'the
system' rules and
people hide behind 'the
practices', or the
procedures or even 'the
culture'?

This is a very simple set of questions to get you started
with your reflections and actions. Use the blank pages to
record your own questions and notes

173

▶ *Your Questions and Notes:*

▶ *Your Questions and Notes:*

The Leader with Seven Faces

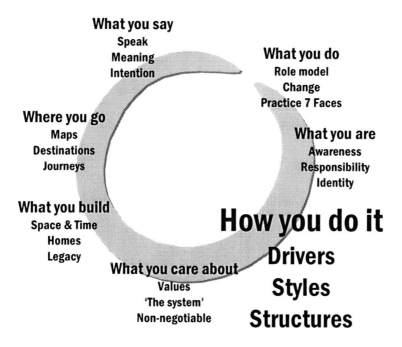

What you say
Speak
Meaning
Intention

What you do
Role model
Change
Practice 7 Faces

Where you go
Maps
Destinations
Journeys

What you are
Awareness
Responsibility
Identity

What you build
Space & Time
Homes
Legacy

How you do it
Drivers
Styles
Structures

What you care about
Values
'The system'
Non-negotiable

The Leader with Seven Faces

5

How you do it
Drivers
Styles
Structures

"A true leader has the confidence to stand alone, the courage to make tough decisions, and the compassion to listen to the needs of others. He does not set out to be a leader, but becomes one by the quality of his actions and the integrity of his intent."

Anonymous

This is for many, perhaps including you, 'the real question'. As a leader, one could easily get excited with (or lost in) the rhetoric, confess good organization-building intentions, think of a leadership legacy, provide good maps for the troops, profess a value system, 'do' great things, be emotionally aware of what's happing to oneself and the organization…but have a style of 'doing' that screws up everything!

You may have been part of management meetings where the facilitator wants to focus the group on 'what' needs to be done, announcing that the 'how' is not what matters, that this is something you will figure out later. In other words, get the 'what' right and the 'how' will follow. I have always had an enormous discomfort with this kind of thinking that splits these two. I understand the principle of the focus, but I also know that many good 'what' issues get killed by their 'how', and that many good 'how' discussions help refine the original 'what' or even question it!

The three themes for this face of the leader - in which the focus is on the 'how to do things' - are:

- **Drivers:** The 'how' is determined by what drives the leader. What drives the leader is often determined by what he measures! Yes, it should be the other way around, but very often it isn't! What we measure matters so much that it will be a good starting point for this conversation.

- **Styles:** We could spend a lot of time on classifications and styles-of-quality lists. There are many of them around, and many of them are also 'good maps'. I would like you to pay far less attention to a particular label-style, but more to the discovery of your own style - the leader's style - and its implications.

- **Structures:** I will not lead you into the discussion of the thousand-and-one variations of organizational models and charts. I'd like to propose a more philosophical discussion and view of what I call 'degrees of freedom' and models of collaboration. This 'how' is far more relevant than the mapping of a series of reporting lines.

Drivers

A traditional view of the organizational focus is the one that distinguishes between ('satisfaction of') customers, shareholders, employees and other stakeholders (society?).

Another traditional view is the one supported by the *I-want-it-all-because-everything-is-important* school of management. That school solves 'the problem' of where to start. If you started with a blank statement saying that the organization is there to 'maximize shareholder value' and you were challenged – for example, what about the employees? - the answer would be, well, employees will only gain if shareholders are satisfied. If you put the customer first, you can use a similar argument: only if the customers are satisfied, the shareholders will be.

In the modern 21st century environment, the dispute for the first slot in the mission statements is usually the one between 'customer' and 'shareholders' Few companies (with shareholders) tend to put employees first. This is usually seen as a nice-but-unrealistic approach that doesn't deal with the realities of the market (customer satisfaction, shareholder satisfaction). A well-publicized exception is Southwest Airlines, where you can find a declaration of the sort, "*Sorry customer, but you come second.*"

Where you start, what you include, what you omit, matters and very often explains the drivers. This leadership decision defines the focus of attention, language, external image and people's expectations. But, far more important than what missions, visions and other declarations say, is often the question of what's happening in the reality of day–to-day life.

And the best way to analyse this is to look at the measurement systems in place.

▶ Measuring

This issue of measurement is crucial because it influences and contaminates the leadership thinking. Your business education and experience tells you that 'if you can't measure it, you can't manage it'. Your boss asked you yesterday for 'the numbers' in your predictions, and in the last management team meeting that you attended you spent a fair amount of time discussing 'how are we going to know that we have succeeded, how are we going to measure it'?

Good managers and leaders are sometimes defined by their ability to measure outcomes and performance. Bad managers and leaders often by their weakness and apparent vagueness in describing what needs to be achieved. Some sort of numbers, ratios, scales, 'data' is expected. Free-floating descriptions of outcomes based upon 'qualities' or 'feelings' are considered week, fuzzy, unimportant. That is, of course, unless you can translate them into 'numbers'. Numbers give us comfort; their absence produces some anxiety and fuels uncertainty. Measurements are part of life and numbers are part of measurement.

Measurement Theory tells us there is more than one way to do it. How many children you have is an absolute measurement; the word three or four means precisely that. Nominal measurements assign numbers to things (or people): you are employee 3467, and nobody else is. Your Christian name has been transformed into a number, 564309, because payroll computers don't like names, and, besides, they embarrass everybody confusing Cristina, Christine, Christian and Christienne…because the programmer who designed the thing only allowed for the six first characters – his name is Bob.

All relative and utility theory is based upon the premise that if a is bigger than b and b is bigger that c, then, a is always bigger than c. Similarly, if you prefer a to b and b to c, then surely you must prefer a to c. The brain has trouble with absolutes, but understands very well that this is hotter than that, and that this stick is shorter than that one. Fahrenheit associated 'one degree' with the ability of the brain to distinguish and differentiate between two temperatures. We grasp differences between things better than we understand their absolute properties. Ordinal measurement such as A, B, C academic grades allows us to mentally classify life. We all know what 'to be number 1' means in almost any circumstance. It works for market positioning as well as for the hardness of minerals. There are other ingredients in the measurement cookbook, such as 'interval' and 'ratios'.

▶ *Managing ratios*

This short but deliberate promenade into the world of measurement is just to say that…you can't escape measurement and you can't escape numbers. But measurements are arbitrary navigators for the brain, a means to understand reality and make some sense of order, priorities, relative differences, risks, dangers, volume, etc. They do not constitute an end in themselves. The ratio 'money spent on training per employee' is a means to understand and track (measure) what management is doing for the skills-development of staff, something that presumably they are committed to. Leaders are committed to the staff, to the skill pool and to the investment in training, not to the ratio in itself! Agree? Well, the trouble is that many leaders behave as managers of ratios, instead of leaders of people and processes.

The indicator easily becomes 'the target' to manage if one is not careful, such is the pressure on measuring and the way it is embedded in daily life. 'Earnings per share' (EPS) means exactly that: a ratio, an indicator of how much you have earned per each share you hold. It is straightforward and far from sexy. It is supposed to indicate how well the company has done financially so that the shareholder gets his investment back. That's it. However, entire corporations are run as if EPS were the only thing to talk about, the *raison d'être*, the only visible measure and the only one you should care about, as dictated by the City/Wall Street.

A CEO standing in front of the workforce congratulating them for the increase of 0.55 cents in EPS above the market expectation, should be offered a session either at an optician or a psychiatrist, depending on your benevolence. It is insulting to say the least to reduce the commitment, achievements, long hours, tribulations, creativity, discoveries, efforts, anxiety, excitement, love for the organization, frustrations and innovation put into the company to a 0.55 EPS increase. That CEO confuses thermometer with fever, degrees of temperature with sweating and mercury bars with infection. The ratio - like the mercury bar - has no soul. Individuals (and organizations) do.

► *Reality in a jacket*

But it would be easy to blame *wallstreetnomics* for their numerical addiction and the leaders of the corporation for using an artefact that is part of a navigator system for people. Measurement seems to have become *the* reality around us. It is embedded in education, in the culture and in most of 'Western' language. I once stood in front of a beautiful new bridge, linking two equally beautiful parts of land. The bridge was the crème de la crème of engineering and it had managed to create an even more beautiful landscape. It was described by the guide as a '30 million, three km long, three-year construction, 40-tons' bridge, followed by all possible statistics on numbers of people and cars. Even the volume of paint used was quoted. He could not answer any questions as to why it was there, who built it, how people on both sides felt or any other emotional repertoire about the place. The bridge was a set of numbers. Over the years, I have heard exactly the same about cathedrals, houses, farms, stadiums, rivers or even a South African bush camp. "*Give me the numbers!*" society seems to shout.

Students of psychology used to hear that 'intelligence is whatever is measured by an intelligence test'. It was intended to be a joke, but it isn't. That's it; you *are* 150 I.Q. or 75 I.Q. as measured by the broadly accepted test. In a parallel way, reality is whatever it deserves to be allocated by our measurement system.

Years ago, I learnt from the head of news of the BBC how they 'classified' the news. Something, somewhere is happening and immediately it becomes a 'two-camera, two crew, three-day news item' or 'a one-camera, two reporters, one-day news item', etc. How it's going to be encapsulated and *straightjacketed* is a measure of the importance, relevance and amount of resources that reality deserves. Something *is* 'front page' or 'page five', or 'quarter of a column' in the same way as your job *is* a 75K, a 25K or a 100K – whether that's in dollars, pounds or any other currency. It's terribly pragmatic as communication tool (!) and 'it works'.

But measurement almost as an end in itself is pervasive. It has the toxic ability of creating a new reality in itself that completely takes over the one it's supposed to serve. It's an argument as old as the philosophical discussions between nominalism (universal principles such as redness or tallness only exist in particular things), realism (tallness and redness do exist in themselves without any reference to things) and conceptualism (it's all in your mind, it's abstract). Managerial Philosophy has not been invented, I know, but I wonder whether the financial analysts that believe that EPS *does* exist (*"Hello EPS, how are you today,"* I suppose) would qualify as founders or members of the Wall Street Realism School.

▶ *Digression one: a social example*

I was trained as a psychiatrist and practiced as such for more than fifteen years. In those days, the classification of mental disorders was in tatters and heavily contaminated by a history of wars between schools of thought and approaches. Pharmacology (the science of drugs), however, was growing. Since 1952 it had become clear that one could significantly modify serious mental illness with new drugs called psychotrops. The 60s brought the antidepressants almost by serendipity and the 70s saw a massive deployment of drug clinical trials in areas that traditional medicine had discounted for serious research. 'Having a peptic ulcer or not' as a descriptive entry criterion for a drug trial was clear-cut, 'having depression' was not!

People carrying out clinical trials with these new powerful drugs needed to make sure that whatever it was they were targeting, it was *'operationalized'* enough to ensure that the groups of patients would be homogeneous, that they were similar in their characteristics. Their goal was what is called 'reliability'. They cared less about how that 'target population' (the groups of patients enrolled) was or wasn't, say, the 'real depression', than about the fact that all those 100 patients enrolled complied with the same criteria. In other words, in methodological terms, their goal wasn't 'validity'; their interest was 'reliability'.

They were happy to trade off one for the other. They were not in the business of 'understanding' depression, but of grasping and measuring a set of symptoms that - appearing in clusters in populations usually called 'depressed' - seemed to represent that illness. And to be fair to them, as good researchers, they never hid that. Psychopharmacology - the science that studies the drugs that are able to modify brain functioning and mental states - boomed. Suddenly, dozens of well-thought-out 'research diagnostic criteria (RDC)' (as they were rightly called) were born in the USA. Their use was pervasive and invaded normal, non-experimental, non-clinical trial clinical practice. If it was good for drug trials, surely, it must be good for day-to-day ward rounds in hospitals, people seemed to think. At the back of those RDC, a full classification of 'real diseases' was born, called 'Diagnostic

Criteria' and the US manuals (DSM-III, DSM-IV) became pretty much 'THE book' that medical residents consulted (and consult!) to establish a clinical (I repeat, clinical!) diagnosis.

In the pockets of the white coats of the medical psychiatrics residents and interns, there was now a single little abbreviated book starting with the letters DSM (Diagnostic and Statistic Criteria). Those new definitions of diseases were miles away from the old-fashioned, fuzzy, un-graspable concepts of just a decade ago. Now, to be qualified as a 'major depression', for example, patients should have nine or ten of those symptoms, not have such and such, and exhibit those for more than, say, a month. It was called by some the Chinese menu system of diagnostic: a bit of this, a bit of that, that's called chicken Cantonese-style. One of this, three of those, that's a depression. It was, and it is, extremely successful.

The US classification of mental disorders now rules the waves beyond Manhattan and the Golden Gate. The system has been translated into almost any language with very little work on the 'local validation'. In this system, the combination of such and such symptom, plus this one, plus that one, not having this and that, and complaining for this period of time, *is* depression, or *is* schizophrenia, or *is* anxiety. They do not represent them or indicate them, they simply *are*. It's drug-therapy-realism. American Psychiatry has been carried away by the success and now all sorts of 'new entities' have been described in the same way, growing the number of 'medical conditions' Chinese-menu style. The risk of *'medicalization'* of non-medical situations is as high as ever, but the beauty of the operational criteria is winning.

I have taken you on this long digression into mental illness for several reasons. In part, because I am taking the liberty of using my educational bias (!); in part, because this issue of the 'growing-like-mushrooms, new medical/psychiatric entities treatable by drugs' is in the news a lot these days (reasonable people becoming suspicious of the drug companies' influence); and partly because it is a real life social example of 'quantification-measurement-need for encapsulating the reality in statistical frames' that is creating a reality of its own.

▶ *Digression two: education, hospitals, league tables.*

Another social example is educational. It has been described as the *teach-to-the-test* problem. In some educational systems, testing has become an end in its own right, so that we can have comparative league tables, for example. There are preparations for the test, mock-ups, predictions and finally, the tests. In this collective frame of mind, passing the test or answering the questions becomes the driver. The understanding behind it, is not. In some schools, 'normal teaching' stops at some points to 'prepare for the exams'. That is not about enhancing a cognitive understanding of the topic, but maximizing the chances of a good mark. These two things are not the same. You would have thought that they are linked, but the gap is widening.

Recent studies in the UK - that started on the academic side, but that were progressively and reluctantly acknowledged by the government - show that 'teaching to the test' is damaging overall education.

Healthcare management is also full of similar situations where performance measurement has become coterminous with efficiency and good practice. Some examples in the UK healthcare system have gone that way. For example, trying to decrease waiting list times. Waiting list time in some cases has decreased, but with other unintended consequences for (or negative impact on) other services.

Another example, the goal 'you should be able to see your General Practitioner within 48 hours' has the logical 'measurement' attached. For physician practices to meet those targets, they need to keep open spaces in a 48-hour period for those requesting a visit. Doing so, meant that anybody wanting to book an appointment for, say, one month from now, was rejected and told to come back 'within 48 hours of when the appointment was needed' (what else?). When the British Prime Minister, Tony Blair, was challenged in an interview about this practice, he first referred to the-good-intentions-behind-this, but then immediately switching - possibly thanks to the remaining party-politics-uncontaminated sector of his brain - to acknowledge that it was nonsense (and, incidentally, a nonsense that he wasn't aware of!)

▶ *Bring on the numbers!*

At the time of writing, political discourse in the United Kingdom is reaching levels of socially engineered boredom and progressive alienation from the younger generation. Politicians addressing the news have been programmed by PR, political marketers and communication machineries to regurgitate statistics no matter what:

"What do you think of the risk posed by the avian flu?"

"Well, since we have been in power, 3000 more nurses have been hired, there are 4000 extra specialists, we have increased hospital capacity by 2000 beds, more money has gone into the NHS than in previous governments, we have allocated £340 million of 'new money' (a buzzword for money not allocated somewhere else in the budget) *and total investment has gone up by 25% in real terms."*

"But, how much do we know about avian flu and the risk for our country?"

"We recognize that this is a challenge for all of us in the West but, the important thing is to recognize that, since we have been in power, 3000 more nurses have been hired, there are 4000 extra specialists, we have increased hospital capacity by 2000 beds, more money has gone into the NHS than in previous governments, we have allocated £340 million of 'new money' and total investment has gone up by 25% in real terms."

"On another topic, what do you think of the anti-war demonstrations?"

"Well, as you know, this is not my department but let me say one thing. People are entitled to express their opinions as they usually do with the Health Service. It is important to remember that since we have been in power, 3000 more nurses have been hired, there are 4000 extra specialists, we have increased hospital capacity by 2000 beds, more money has gone into the NHS than in previous governments, we have

allocated £340 million of 'new money' and total investment has gone up by 25% in real terms."

If you think that I am just exaggerating, you probably don't live in the UK.

▶ *Prisoners of the numbers*

The comfort of measurement is unquestionable. If we can frame a reality, put some borders around it, define the limits and measure some attributes, we feel we 'know' that reality. That's life. Not surprising then, that management and leadership of organizations, as part of that life, are only translating into their practices what seems to be an otherwise normal way to navigate life. In many areas of management today, many things would not be taking seriously (read: qualify for funding) if their Return on Investment (ROI) couldn't be measured. Like my ex-colleagues in psychiatry believe, it seems as if having a number (it has been measured) is good enough. Never mind that the number has been cooked up via clever arithmetic.

A few years ago, a typical topic in the area of so–called 'knowledge management' (KM) was the measurement of the ROI of any KM initiative.

"We'd love to have a total Information Management System 'system', but you have to show us its ROI first."
"Do you want an ROI? Yes sir, you'll have it."

And alas, here it comes. Telling us that people, for example, will not waste 127 hours looking for the information they want (because they'll have it at their fingertips), thus speeding up the quest for finding an answer by 1.35 months, which can be translated into a 2-month reduction in product development plans. Multiply that by the average wage, by the expected revenues. *"Here you are, Sir, this is the greatest ROI ever. You'll spend $2M on the system but you will get $30M extra sales, so what do you think?"*

Well, I'll tell you what I think! If you discount the employees who surf the net for fun; multiply that by an absenteeism coefficient (which I have just invented) and by the probability of getting information that you don't need; minus a 'bad weather modification ratio' (which I will be happy to describe); then multiply that by the probability of success of your IT department ever getting the damn thing to work and discounting the reduction in product development time that was going to happen *anyway* because you have just dropped the latest phase study; that gives you an ROI of $2.50 which equals 5 lollypops of $0.50. So, what do you think of that?

I have seen ridiculous ROIs that have gone down extremely well with management, just because they were done and were called ROI and looked good. I have seen good potential drugs stopped in their development within pharmaceutical companies because their Net Present Value (NPV) was pathetic according to secret calculations done on the 10th floor by market research and strategic marketing. Only to be resuscitated the following year after the market predictions had miraculously changed and several new twists on the 10th floor had made the whole thing now very NPV-attractive. The accuracy of 'Peak Sales' forecast in some companies looks pretty much like $500M, plus or minus $200M. However, project portfolio managers make decisions based on those calculations. 'Big prospective sales' would be unacceptable, $235M is acceptable, but both may share equal solidity.

I have seen pricing strategies presented in a 6kg-heavy ring binder (with a several hundred thousand dollar consulting bill attached) that reaches the conclusion that you should market something at $6 a pack, only to be thrown out by management who said, "*I think it's $7.50.*" I don't think the latter was less solid. A friend of mind used to have an open dinner invitation for anybody who could unequivocally prove that any performance forecast by Strategic Planning (be it peak sales, market share or NPV achievement) had ever been hit. To my knowledge, he has never invited anybody yet.

"Do you want numbers, sir? Sure, you'll have them," we seem to profess. Forget sophisticated decision analytical models, give me a calculator and a back of an envelope and I will justify anything under the magic sponsorship of the number.

So, let's abandon the numbers! Well, I hope you don't read something this naïve between the lines. But leadership in organizations is in desperate need of questioning the reality that is very often hidden under hundreds of ratios, indicators, and other surrogate mirrors. Leadership is in desperate search of judgement and meaning. 'Managing the numbers' is bad management; managing with numbers is needed. Reality is not its measurement. The measurement is supposed to help us navigate through reality. Leadership is often hijacked by the metrics, but at the same time it desperately needs them. The whole area of 'performance indicators' of one sort or another - including the attempt to measure some intangibles such as 'commitment', for example - is fascinating. The winners will be the ones who come up with innovative measures, probably surrogates, or surrogates of a surrogate, and at the same time present and voice them *as such.*

My own secret rule of thumb is that leadership strength inversely correlates with the amount of numbers the leader presents or talks about. If you can only speak about numbers, what kind of leader are you, people often seem to say. If you lead by number, the numbers will lead you and the organization behind you. Your choice.

▶ Benchmarking the future?

Forget benchmarking. At best, let yourself be benchmarked. If you have benchmarking as a key strategic driver, in the best case scenario you will excel at the art of catching up. You will not invent the new breakthrough product, create a new market or be unique at what you do. Ok, you may want to see your company at the top of the Reality-of-today league table. If this is what you want, fine.

Benchmarking is a form of comparison with the so-called best practices. Typically, a company does the research for you, within your industry, following pre-defined parameters and measures, so you are eventually able to compare yourself with your competitors. It could be a productivity comparison, a quality comparison or, simply, some form of performance comparison with others on what you do. Assuming that the research is done thoroughly and that people are not trying to compare apples with pears, you will have any statistic you want and you will put yourself somewhere in the spectrum between bad and good. League tables in schools and hospitals in Britain and other countries are a form of benchmarking

The problem with benchmarking is that sometimes people spend extraordinary efforts comparing themselves with others based on a reality that is gone: the past. It is impossible to benchmark yourself against things that have not happened yet. The future is not *benchmarkable*. Benchmarking is catching up. It is rear-view mirror management, not future development. Leaders who are obsessed with benchmarking are like those huge American lorries with those huge, prominent rear-view mirrors that look more like airplane wings.

Benchmarking also has the potential to block creativity since the efforts are focused on what is happening or has happened as opposed to what may happen in the future. Benchmarking is loved by leaders of the inevitable, leaders whose main priority in business is to lead things that otherwise would happen anyway. Leaders should be paid for driving things that would not happen unless they were there. Organizations that put too much emphasis on benchmarking may miss the innovation train. Since benchmarking needs today's data (or, to be more precise, yesterday's) it may produce tunnel vision, the least visionary of visions!

I wonder whether Bill Gates, founder of Microsoft, was 'benchmarking' when in 1985 he stated that 640K of computer memory ought to be enough for anybody. Obviously, it was not benchmarking that saved him from this 'vision'. Kenneth Olsen, co-founder of the computer company Digital Equipment Corporation, was also 'benchmarking' when in 1977 he said there was no reason why anyone would want a computer in their home. Surely, the benchmarking consultants of the day could not find any computer in any home, so the hypothetical benchmarking study would have confirmed the reality that could support Mr Olsen's views.

In 1876, Sir William Preece, Chief Engineer of the British Post Office did his own benchmarking (although he did not know the term!) and argued that *"The Americans have need for the telephone but we do not. We have plenty of messenger boys."* Probably the imaginary benchmarking research of the day would have produced a league table of 'fast to slow messengers'.

DECCA, the record company, must also have been benchmarking the musical market when they rejected the Beatles on the grounds that guitar music was 'on the way out'. I don't know, but I bet they even had 'hard statistical data'!

Business history is full of examples where true innovation defies the expectations of today and the realities of the past. I can't think of a benchmarking consultant doing research for Sony and (a) finding that people wanted to have little battery-powered boxes hanging from their belts with thin wires hooked into their ears, playing music on the street on their way to the office or (b) they actually found examples of that strange behaviour in the market and reported the competitors' facts to Sony. The walkman was not invented on the back of benchmarking (or market research for that matter).

► *Leading incrementalism*

Benchmarking usually leads to an incrementalist mentality. If one is behind on something, surely by putting into practice some measures, one can advance one, three, five points etc. Benchmarking is a race against somebody who has already won. Nicholas Negroponte, of the MIT Media Labs is quoted to say that *"incrementalism is innovation's worst enemy."* I agree.

Is benchmarking such a waste? No. Like many things in life it depends on how seriously you take the exercise and the data. If benchmarking data is used to generate ideas, to make wake-up calls when things are not great, or simply to understand what's going on in your world, then you should welcome it. But to make benchmarking into a sort of religion or, indeed, as in many organizations, the driver for strategy, is a waste of time. If you find a company you know or, say, a potential employer singing the benchmarking song as the main theme, I suggest you downgrade your expectations.

Entire change management programmes in organizations are based upon some form of benchmarking, even when the term is not used. You can see those drivers: industry standards, averages of competitors' performances, constant reference to 'industry best practices', etc. Those approaches are unlikely to produce radical change. By that I mean sustainable change that is not incremental and that leads the organization to a next, higher level of possibilities. Some change programmes are based on a simple extrapolation of the past and present, containing a horizon that is a sort of 'better picture' of today.

To be fair to benchmarking addicts, many books, publications and conferences that contain benchmarking in the title are using the term in the broadest way: a panorama of what is around or available today. In the best case, a journalistic account of management practices that organizations have put into place and the benefits they have achieved under such and such programme. Strictly speaking, this is not benchmarking but an exposure of 'practices' often presented without much judgement. The word 'best' associated with the title ('best practices') does not guarantee to me that what you see is any 'best'.

► Leading from ignorance

The fact that many entrepreneurial ventures are often led by people who knew little about that industry, tells you that they were unlikely to rely on benchmarking data or industry standards to produce something different. This is, of course, not always the case. But certainly the most successful and lasting entrepreneurial enterprises produce something 'different' or 'unique'. Not better, but something that was probably unpredictable.

In 1976, a professor of economics, Muhammad Yunus, had the 'wild' idea of creating a bank that lends relatively small amounts to the poor and to the sector of the population in his world with less access to money: women. The Grameen Bank was created. Today, they reach millions of borrowers. It has become a very successful enterprise with minimum levels of defaults, and which is now extended to other services, for example, mobile communications. The 'Grameen model' has certainly led to successful enterprises outside banking, let alone the intrinsic merit as a socially responsible initiative. I am pretty sure that professor Yunus did not rely on benchmarking data (or 'banking best practices') to find the initiative in the chapter 'lending to the poor, to women and to people who will never repay'. What he did was against any standard 'best banking practice'. In reality, he put into practice the 'worst possible practice'.

History of mankind, history of business, history of ideas: all are full of predictions that were wrong and that - had they been fully followed - would have blocked innovation. All of them have in common the focus on the present or the past, a rear-view mirror strategy or benchmarking-like motivation. Lord Kelvin, past President of the prestigious Royal Society (UK), predicted in 1895 that flying machines heavier than air were impossible. A few years later, in 1923, Robert Millikan, winner of the Nobel Prize for Physics, predicted that *"there is no likelihood that man can ever tap the power of the atom"*. 20 years later, the founder of IBM, Thomas Watson, stated that *"there is a world market for maybe five computers"*. Perhaps the most striking statement in the history of complacency (and arrogance) comes from the often quoted Charles H. Duell, U.S. Commissioner of Patents, who in 1899 recommended the abolishment of the Patent Office on the grounds that *"everything that can be invented, has been invented"*.

What has always interested me is that you can hardly find idiots amongst the pool of people stating those (today seen as ridiculous) things. I.Q. must surely not correlate with 'business predictions'!

Benchmarking should, in the best of cases, be a starting point, not an aim in itself. A platform for conversation and for moving forward; data to reflect upon and forget quickly. Innovation comes from exploring the unthinkable, from stretching the world of possibilities, from a healthy *"forget benchmarking, what if we did this?"* Out-of-the-box thinking is needed more than benchmarking data. The problem with out-of-he-box thinking is that it is often in short supply in semi-bureaucratic and super-structured environments.

I sometimes use a vignette of a group of managers who are discussing 'out-of–the-box thinking' to illustrate these difficulties. One of them is addressing the others and saying: *"In my department, we are encountering some difficulties with thinking out-of-the-box. We have had a series of meetings discussing the size of the box, the need for a box, the market availability of boxes and our own benchmarking data on boxes. We don't seem to agree on many things yet, but we are progressing towards the next stage where we will address the issues of what materials the box should be constructed from, a budget for the box and our first choice of box vendors."*

Leadership by numbers, by ratios, by benchmarking, or combinations thereof, is risky business. Organizations that boost a measurement-fundamentalist ethos and generate their leaders accordingly, miss the point. When the drivers of leaderships are numbers, their language hijacks the reality and there is no room for anything else.

Styles

Another dimension of this 'how you do it' leadership is often called style. You'll find no shortage of labels to describe these and I am not going to suggest a list to you. But I have always been fascinated by a particular style that I have seen again and again on both sides, as employee and consultant. I have called it 'toxic leadership' because it has a tremendous ability to inject social toxicity into the organization.

▶ *10 ways to kill an organization*

I am talking here about sophisticated murder, perfect crime, Alfred Hitchcock style. Not the arson in corporate headquarters or even the disappearance of the company into history via a merger and acquisition that perhaps merged nothing and acquired all. I am talking about the subtle intoxication of the organization that goes largely unnoticed by many and is perhaps only slightly suspected by some. I am talking about slow poisoning perpetrated by expert assassins with a hidden agenda. I am talking about a thriller script of the type where husband poisons wife with small doses of cyanide provided under the guise of caring for her. In some organizations it's not that difficult to identify prime suspects. In fact, you may even know them well and, to be more precise, you may even report to them. There are two types of Toxic Leaders, the obvious obnoxious and the caring ones. One of them is very dangerous. That's right, the one who cares and poisons under the guise of care.

I offer 10 scripts, sketches for an organizational thriller of the kind described above. You can choose the heroes and villains you want - I just lend you the script. You also get to choose the extras and the location. I'll be the producer. If you get back to me with a developed script – obviously, you wouldn't expect me to give you anything other than the idea for free! – we'll try Hollywood first and we'll share the profits. Alternatively, we may try Business Schools: the case study industry is doing well and, quite frankly, anything is better than the Toyota penetration of the US market and the ultimate maximization of shareholder value in the rise and fall of the car industry in Southern California.

- Leadership Script 1: "*I just know*"
  Subtitle: "*I just know that we'll do x, but let the team go and explore options*"

The senior leader not only openly relies on teams but declares himself the Great Defender of the Team Spirit. He nurtures them and protects them. He has a point of personally coaching all the Project Leaders, which is received with mixed feelings. He encourages the teams to explore possibilities and scenarios, to be open minded and see the big picture. But he …'just knows what is going to happen'. Confronted with a problem, he asks for ideas to explore although 'he knows the answer'. Pattern repeated several times, eventually meets with suspicion from the teams that feel they are wasting their time and the Big Guy is just playing ego. By the time the toxicity has come out into the open, half of the project leaders have left in the pursuit of a boss who 'knows less' and the other half is either bored or enjoying stock options.

- Leadership Script 2: "*Let them fail*"
  Subtitle: "*Wrong path but they need to see it for themselves*"

The 'Let Them Fail' script is practised in paternalistic and patronizing organizations where the seniors have chronically mistaken a business organization for a primary school. 'Let them fail' toxicity is very subtle because it's practised under the guise of a 'learning environment' where people 'learn by mistakes' and are 'empowered to take risks'. Suspicions come up halfway through the script when some people who failed were fired. Script ends with people having a great laugh the next time the CEO speaks highly about Knowledge Management whilst collecting the Learning Organization of the Year Award.

- Leadership Script 3: "*Try harder*"
  Subtitle: "*Guess what I want*"

Teams are never 'quite there' when presenting results of the 3-month analysis of the problem and go back time and again to refine their exploration. Suspicion arises when after a few reiterations a Project Leader has a revelation and asks, "*Why don't you tell us what you want? That would save us from trying harder every time and 'going back to the team'.*" That same Project Leader has pathetic annual performance reviews and leaves the organization to teach a motivation course in high school. Other colleagues reinvent Scenario Planning, not focused on market conditions or competitor intelligence but on the boss' beliefs. Project Teams rename the Project Leader as 'Project Detective' in order to guess what senior management wants.

- Leadership Script 4: "*I have the answer, what's the question?*"
  Subtitle: "*Been there, done that, trust me I know!*"

A slight variation of script 1, this organization is governed by leaders who are looking back in time and refer constantly to their previous experiences. In a change management programme, they bring the McKinsey templates from their last company's M&A to the first start up meeting. The answers are there and they have them. In an HR problem, they are super-psychologists with answers. For a financial problem, they have the answer because they have been there before. Reality is pretty much 'mapped' and staff switches off creativity because it's useless around the place. Sudden death occurs in this script when market conditions change drastically and the application of the combined wisdom of all the experienced leaders kills the company through lack of new ideas and imagination.

- Leadership Script 5: "*Legitimized suicide*"
  Subtitle: "*You decide who is redundant - this is a very humane M&A*"

In this script, M&A consulting gurus decide that it's better to leave the staff to decide who will survive, rather than to burden the leadership team with such an inhumane decision. Division Heads are gathered and handed a Business Plan and a timetable. Following some sleepless nights, a good third of them, managers and staff, have decided they will be redundant in the new, merged company, so they should leave. The trick in this script is that there is no visible murderer and that a proportion of staff dies via collective suicide whilst singing,

"What a wonderful humane death this is." Close to the end, a twist: two surviving division heads blame the leadership team for plainly abdicating their responsibilities as leaders and dressing up the whole thing as a democratic decision. CEO ends the script by highlighting this case as an example of how humane, democratic and open the company is.

- Leadership Script 6: *"Do, but don't do"*
  Subtitle: *"Feel free to do, but make sure that we tell you what to do"*

This script takes place in a very 'free environment' where people are encouraged to take initiatives of all sorts, to take action. Examples are numerous. On one occasion at the peak of the script, a manager goes out of her way to implement a programme that she felt she had been encouraged to do. To her surprise, she is reprimanded and de facto demoted because she wasn't supposed to go that way. Puzzled and frustrated she leaves. Colleagues demand an explanation but don't get very far. She was supposed to know what she shouldn't do despite the fact that she had done exactly what she had been suggested to do by the same supervisor who had reprimanded her. Script ends with highlights of collective frustration when it's discovered that this pattern of 'do it, but don't do it' is very common across the board. One manager leaves after making a documentary on Mental Health in the Work Place and selling the rights to The Institute of Psychiatry.

- Leadership Script 7: "*You are empowered to believe me*"
  Subtitle: "*We are all empowered, but I am more empowered than others*"

This script borrows heavily from "*we are all equal, but some of us are more equal than others*" but translates it into empowerment. Empowerment is a heavily used buzzword in that organization and figures prominently in the mission statement. Life is relatively peaceful until a manager asks the question, "*What does it mean?*" Infuriated senior leader responds with a long sermon on trust, culture, values and principles. Small guy asks again, "*But what does it mean to be empowered?*" Big guy says, "*Look how empowered I am by the Board*". Script goes on and on. Graffiti starts to appear on walls, doors and toilet partitions with unpleasant statements about the credibility of the company rhetoric. Organization slowly dies of buzzword intoxication.

- Leadership Script 8: "*Maximum accountability, minimum authority*"
  Subtitle: "*Great titles, great visibility, great blindness*"

In this organization, accountabilities are very well-defined – a very rare event in itself which makes the script automatically qualify as part of the 'New Ideas Movement'. Everybody knows quite well what he or she is accountable for. Hidden, small quantity toxicity comes from providing everybody with the impression that they possess the accompanying authority. But this is simply not true. Authority lies somewhere else, usually with people not very accountable for anything other than accumulating as much authority as possible. Leaders' egos are boosted with big 'accountable' titles such as Global

Project Leader (a company equivalent of UN Secretary General). Only a few soon discover they have no real authority to act and they escape shortly after. The ones that are trapped become blind. The Big Titles practice game eventually falls apart when more and more managers become suspicious of the mismatch in accountability-authority. CEO responds by creating a new layer of highly accountable managers with very sexy titles on their business cards.

- Leadership Script 9: "*Great goals & future, great cuts*"
  Subtitle: "*We are doing well but you are fired*"

Organization is doing well, growth has been declared, annual results are not bad. CEO proclaims new stage of high hopes and possibilities. Almost in parallel, R&D is cut by 20% and those in the wrong place at the wrong time are fired, regardless of their talents. Many people question the consistency behind the actions but this is rapidly dismissed by leadership as lack of business strategy understanding. The pattern repeats itself several times during the script so that a pavlovian reflex begins to occur: every time the CEO declares, "*Good year, excellent results, we need to grow*", staff trembles.

- Leadership Script 10: "*Frog boiling*"
  Subtitle: "*There are two ways to boil a frog and you should be feeling a bit warm by now*"

This script is based upon the tale 'There are two ways to boil a frog'. One is to have a container with boiling water and throw the frog in. The frog burns himself but jumps out quickly as a reflex and survives. The other way is to throw the frog into a recipient with cold water and switch the heat on. The frog is very happy feeling the progressive warm and cosy environment until he's boiled without him noticing it. This script is offered for free interpretations and applications in the life of managers in organizations.

■ Leadership Script 11

Script 11 – mathematics have never been my forte! – is based on the combination of the other 10. In this script, leaders believe that all of the above are a bit of a joke, entertainment, a light way to cover a few topics, nothing serious, no terribly elaborated ideas, certainly not a reflection of real life, funny stories, amusement disguised as management thinking. Readers in script 11 mode perhaps feel rather warm and cosy. Please check that the heat is off.

► *Brok(lead)ers or Lead(brok)ers*

There is one style of leadership, or 'how you do it' dimension, that I believe has been underplayed and should be higher in any organizational agenda. It is their role as brokers.

A broker in its original sense, and according to the Oxford dictionary, is somebody who buys and sells goods or assets for others. But in its broad sense, a broker is also somebody who acts as intermediary, facilitator, mediator, negotiator or agent; somebody who organizes, orchestrates, settles and brings about plans. In the current information era - where we have long established that the interdependency between people, teams, organizations, divisions, firms, companies and suppliers, customers and companies, and any permutation of those, is enormous - the role of the 'organizational broker' is crucial. I believe that this significantly redefines leadership in the 21st century corporation.

A Senior Leader today must be a Senior Broker. The current business environment doesn't cope well with dictation or command and control. The stereotype of the leadership team beautifully crafting mission statements, leaving the 'implementation' to the troops is dangerous. The troops these days can't function without reference to other troops, starting with the ones that are part of the same company. The interdependence of groups, teams or people is enormous and needs a style of leadership that facilitates the interdependence and collaboration.

Let's look at an example. The enterprise has been re-designed and cut into pieces – now you have Business Units. Or the R&D has become too big and has been split into self-contained organizations. If this is going to work, it will need not only several 'structures' (the Head of the new Business Unit, plus management, plus cast) but also a 'brokerage' structure coordinating them. Otherwise, each of the newly appointed sub-CEOs will go full steam ahead, only concerned by what is good for his/her own Unit. One of the common complaints in the implementation of a 'business unit model' is that *"they don't talk to each other anymore"*, missing the common opportunities and the leverage that the 'single entity' used to provide. The com-plaint is often well-founded. Most of the time, the reason is that there was no brokerage structure in place. The new organization-charts looked slimmer, sexier and fashionable, but nobody actually had a clue as to how to function in this completely different business model.

I suggest that brokerage skills need to come to the rescue in new-economy organizations and be incorporated into the fabric of a modern enterprise, at all leadership levels. If this is so, then surely, at leadership level, it must be part of the intrinsic style and ethos. In the multiple inter-dependent network society of today (external networks with suppliers and customers and other stakeholders; internal networks of teams, divisions, business units, self-contained P&L entities) we need a style of leadership that integrates brokerage as a key ingredient.

▶ The leader of the commons

In this face of leadership, the 'how you do it' face, brokerage skills are crucial. I suspect that the reason why it has been underplayed or underrated is because brokers are often people who work in the background or pull strings from behind without necessarily getting the prominence and air time given to the players. It is like one of those recurrent peace agreements signed on some neutral territory and made possible by the intervention of somebody who you have never heard of. The broker does not steal airtime from the players. Since leaders are usually more visible, it may be that brokerage in the shadows has been counterintuitive!

But for the brokerage model to be successful, the 'function' has to be performed at a senior level. Entire, say, 'Vice-President offices' should be no more than a lean operation with the sole function of making sure that the Business Units talk to each other, that they do not totally compete for the same clients and that they are all making the most of their 'sovereignty' but without the associated cost.

Merged organizations, autonomous business units, split R&D, and parts of the firm competing for limited resources, need brokers who have been trained in *The Tragedy of the Commons*[16]. In this parable, herdsmen use the free pastures of the village commons to feed their animals. The more animals they bring in, the more they can sell. When all the herdsmen think the same way, the tragedy occurs: the commons are overgrazed and destroyed, and there is nothing left for anybody. What starts like the individual 'best interest' leads to a collective loss. The 'tragedy' has been used to discuss pollution, ethical issues, social responsibility, etc. It has now become a semi-compulsory reflection in some primary education programmes in the USA, I have been told. In a broad sense, *The Tragedy of the Commons* means that looking at the world through your own single lenses only - disregarding the world of others - leads to an ugly world for everybody. In leadership terms, if all the 'independents' within the firm (the herdsmen) are left to their own devices, they will seek the maximum return for their business, not caring much for their fellow leaders. Tragedy occurs when they do not talk to each other to ensure that, whatever they do, there is going to be enough pasture (budget, client relationship, priorities...) for everybody. They need a brokerage system that first confronts them with the potential 'tragedy' and then also facilitates the dialogue and the

---

[16] Hardin, Garrett, 1968, *Science* 162, 1243-1248

leverage. Independent units need good external brokers as much as good internal leaders.

Leaders-brokers must have the skills and capabilities to play 'brokerleadership'! They must know how to do what the dictionary says: facilitate, negotiate, orchestrate and mediate. They are leverage-spotters and opportunity-seekers, without being necessarily operationally in charge of any of the 'Units' and with respect for their independence. Leaders-brokers are the guardians of the commons, without owning a single sheep.

Structures

The third dimension of this 'how you do it' face of the leader is what kind of structural fabric is he creating, what kind of ethos, what sort of behavioural DNA? We have addressed the question of 'spaces', 'homes' and 'legacies' in the 'what you build' section. I'd like to propose a different angle here first. Whatever structure, whatever 'organogram', organizations have 'degrees of freedom' and exhibit a particular 'pace' which I describe in terms of *synchronicity* of their people.

► *Surely, you must be jogging*

Imagine a big circular jogging track like the ones you see in big parks and cities, where people go to run on an early morning. You've seen these people many times. Perhaps you are one of them. Big sweat, running shoes, running gear, earphones, etc… I must confess that I have never done it. I am as athletic as an arthritic elephant, but I very much admire all those of you who want to die healthy.

I'd like you to picture three scenarios. One is the 'Random Joggers'. Let's say there are 20 people running on the circular track at any point in time and that they display a normal cross-section of age, ability, physical strength and experience in jogging. They don't know each other (or not all of them) and they run in silence, perhaps just listening to their iPods. In this scenario, people will run more or less at random. A snap picture of the track would tell us that some of them run close together for a while, others are dispersed, some overtake others, some run slowly, some fast, etc. There is no obvious pattern or sense of any synchronicity between them.

The second scenario is 'The Pack'. Here people know each other because they get together to run every day at the same time. They like to run more or less as a group and they chat a bit whilst running. Similar cross-section applies: different abilities, strength, speed capacity, etc. But because they run as a 'pack', some of them will slow down a bit, others will make a bit of an effort to catch up, etc. Some may shout, "*Hey, slow down, guys, I am killing myself.*" Perhaps the core of the pack is engaged in a conversation about last night's TV show. The snap shot picture here is very different: you'll see a group of people relatively close to each other, perhaps two close sub-groups. Even if some people join it at slightly different times, the pack will progressively synchronize and adopt a sort of speed norm or pattern, more or less around the average of what they collectively can do. If this is still too much for somebody every day, he will end up abandoning the pack. The pack may also - consciously or not - 'reject' the ones who are always asking to slow down or who can't catch up with the core.

The third scenario is 'The Race'. The norms here have changed. Maybe the place isn't the friendly track at the park anymore but a proper racing track at the stadium. Let's say the race is about 20 rounds. What do you see? From the start, some may fall behind but the rest doesn't really look random at all. On the contrary, it somehow resembles the pattern of the previous scenario, 'The Pack', but with the silence of the 'Random Joggers' scenario! In other words, no friendly conversations here about last night's TV show. What do they do? The front runner - with the most ability and perhaps the favourite - is not letting himself burn out so he runs fast, defining a sort of pace, but he is certainly not running as fast as he can. The followers are watching him and following him closely, waiting to speed up when he or somebody else starts sprinting and overtaking others. Everybody is depending on everybody else and for a while running at below average (from their potential) speed. If you didn't know that it was a race, you would have thought it's like 'The Pack' because from the outside it looks the same. But of course, this is a temporary illusion until somebody starts to speed up. Then the group disintegrates with some leading, others catching up, others following closely as a 'sub-group' and others definitely lagging behind…

▶ Tracks and pace

In 'The Random Joggers' there is no synchrony amongst the runners. They are driven by their own individual interests of pleasure, having a good time, burning as many calories as possible or running some pre-specified number of miles. 'The Pack' achieves synchrony through the common interest, by people talking to each other or asking others to slow down or saying, "*Come on, let's go faster*". Even if not all members of the pack arrive at the track at the same time, they will synchronize at some point when they find the others. 'The Race' also achieves synchrony through a delicate system of 'watching each other', avoiding burn out, etc. Here, somehow everybody is 'depending' on everybody else from beginning to end.

Now imagine the organization you lead or want to lead as a jogging track where people are participating and giving their mental (and physical!) energy and using/investing their own human capital when 'running'. And the question is: are you/do you want to be on a 'Random Jogging', 'Pack' or 'Race' track?

Your managerial instinct and, possibly, your years of management training or management experience is going to tell you that you are in, or you want to be in, 'the race' model. After all, we all have timelines, objectives, milestones, targets, etc. Your organization does look pretty much like a race many times! Right? Some of you, however, may like the 'pack' model. If nothing else, because there seems to be a lot of 'collaboration' there. Isn't that what your teams are supposed to do? To work as a sort of 'pack'? The 'Random Joggers' model, however, may make you feel that it is too individualistic and chaotic, and that if everybody was like that, it would be impossible to run an organization.

All very well. But suspend your judgment, because the three models have their own merits, and their own liabilities and, as a leader, you need to reflect upon the synchronicity that you are leading or want to lead! There are choices to make!

'The Race' model is appealing because it triggers in us what we have been taught in business schools and business life experience: competition, get there first, watch out what's happening, trick the others (competitors, and not only external but also internal!), reserve yourself, then speed up, run, go, fire, targets, done! However, taking a purely detached, clinical (and cynical) cold view, one could say that, for a big proportion of the duration of the race (the time cycle of the project, or the lifetime of the organization), nobody is making the most of themselves; certainly most of the runners are not using their full capabilities. I know, this is the whole idea of a good race, but take a mathematical approach, not a sports one, not a management one. In this model, for perhaps 90 % of the time, the energy is spent watching and tricking each other.

The 'Pack' model is appealing in managerial terms because it triggers words and feelings such as collaboration, cooperation, people working together, etc. It looks like the equivalent of a team. But, again, there is another side. From a 'clinical' and mathematical viewpoint, 'The Pack' people are synchronizing by paying the price of restricting themselves to the average or to a norm created by that synchronicity. Strictly speaking, in a true 'Pack', people with greater ability will be doing less than they can (but this is the only way to get into that conversation about last night's TV show). Obviously, if they get tired of this, they will either leave the pack (go and work with another more challenging team), run alone (become individualist loose cannons in pursuit of their own agenda) or leave the track altogether (resign, go somewhere else).

The 'Random Joggers' model - which perhaps was intuitively the least appealing when translated into managerial life - however, has the advantage that everybody is theoretically making the most of their own abilities. They are not wasting time and energy accommodating anybody else or watching what others do! But if this is what you want, there is not much team effort or collaboration.

► *Choices*

And this is the crucial point: it all depends on what you want. The scenarios illustrate that you have to accept trade-offs and that the most appealing of organizational models have their own liabilities. Still, many leaders in organizations want to have everything: work as a team, cooperate, make the most of oneself, great individual contributions, get consensus, collaborate, perform to your best abilities, etc. Many leaders run places where race, pack and individual joggers are blurred and they don't see the trade-off between the models.

We see this all the time as well in the way people are recruiting. Places with a heavy 'teamocracy' ethos are not suited for individual joggers. Yet, many recruiting briefings emphasize the individuality (personal background and experience, personal achievements, recognized egos in the market place...) over the ability to fit into a particular company culture. The fiasco soon emerges when the individual jogger (who thought he had been hired for his sprint and demonstrated ability to run very fast) is confronted with a 'Pack' that has norms and consensus below (or above?) his capacity. He had a great CV of sprints and races but little experience in 'packs'. I see this constantly in my consulting work. I also see the same disconnection in the reward system. Leaders praise and promote teamwork but people get rewarded for their individual contributions, etc.

Questions

The 'how you do it' is a very visible face of the leader and deserves serious reflection. It poses questions such as what is driving us and the organization, what kind of styles of leadership are there and what levels of freedom or 'structures'? This is my suggested list of questions, but you are encouraged to consider your own and expand the list!

- Use the list to trigger new questions or to attempt to answer them! Make notes, use the book!
- Commit to one single step to 'answer the question'. These steps may look like actions you want to take, questions you want to ask other people in your organization or 'practice' that you want to do at your next opportunity.

Drivers

- As leader or leader-to-be, how much attention do you pay to the 'how' versus other dimensions? Are you of the type, *"let's fix the what, the how is a detail for later"*? Does it matter?
- Are you leading by numbers? How much of the numbers language is present in your leadership? Are you satisfied? Could you think of making some changes in this area one way or another?
- How do you usually solve the triad 'shareholders, customers, employees' when explaining the focus of the organization? What kind of arguments do you use? Are they consistent with your beliefs? How are they received?

- How much of your leadership style influences the framing of organizational life into measurements? How are measurements serving you? Are you a servant of measurements? Who is winning?
- Are you doing the equivalent of 'teaching-to-the-test'? For example, leading towards milestone achievement but at any cost, no matter what and without any necessary thinking behind it?
- If you ask for ROIs, does this become an end in itself or the key component of decision making? Although there is nothing wrong with this, the question is whether your leadership hides behind triggers such as ROIs or other ratios.
- Are you a prisoner of benchmarking?
- To what extent is your use of benchmarking or 'best practices' as a leader leading the organization towards innovation (versus incrementalism)? Does it matter? How did you make that judgement?

Styles

- Are you an 'I just know' type of leader? Have you or are you projecting that image?
- If you profess to lead or create a 'learning environment', how much do you allow for mistakes? Would you recognize yourself as a sort of 'let them fail' leader?
- Do you lead in 'try harder mode'?
- Are you a leader 'with all the answers'? Even if you say to yourself, "*Of course not!*", would that be seen by others in the same way?
- Do you identify yourself with any other 'toxic leadership' style mentioned?

- How much of a leader-broker are you? Do people come to you for your ability to facilitate, to put people together, to 'glue'? Does it matter? Is this an area that you would like to explore further?
- Do you see yourself as 'leader of the commons'? Would/do people in your organization understand the 'tragedy of the commons' and behave accordingly? That is, not necessarily in their individual self-interest or the sole self-interest of their groups?

Structures

- Are you leading/do you want to lead a 'random jogging', 'pack' or 'race'? Do you see the trade-offs? Are you/ would you lead those trade-offs?
- How much 'synchronicity' do you think there is in your organization? Are you leading in a way that creates a 'structure' of 'regression to the norm' where people tend to accommodate a sort-of-average pace?
- How much of your leadership induces/supports individual contributions and 'pack' styles (teams, collaborations)? Does it matter?
- When interacting with your people, do you prefer the random joggers, the joggers-in-a-pack or the racers? Do you have favourites? Does it matter?
- What kind of 'style of the place' is your leadership fostering?
- What are the 'degrees of freedom' in your people, not necessarily the declared levels of empowerment, but the style of player that your leadership is inducing, consciously or unconsciously?

ACTION MAP
(some first pass questions)

Me   **My organization**

Me

Questions:
What's my area of (metrics) comfort as leader? What's my style? What kind of focus of my leadership (shareholders, consumers, employees)?

Questions:
What are the signals I am sending in terms of what should drive us? Am I one of those 'toxic leaders'? Do I facilitate, dictate, broker?

My organization

Questions:
What would people around me see as my drivers, what style would they see of me?

Questions:
What is the ethos and focus of this organization: Customers, shareholders, employees? What kind of 'pace' do we have (what kind of running tracks) and what are the implications?

This is a very simple set of questions to get you started
In your reflections and actions. Use the blank pages to
record your own questions and notes

▶ *Your Questions and Notes:*

▶ *Your Questions and Notes:*

The Leader with Seven Faces

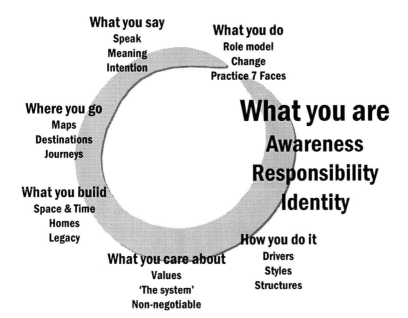

What you say
Speak
Meaning
Intention

What you do
Role model
Change
Practice 7 Faces

Where you go
Maps
Destinations
Journeys

What you are
Awareness
Responsibility
Identity

What you build
Space & Time
Homes
Legacy

How you do it
Drivers
Styles
Structures

What you care about
Values
'The system'
Non-negotiable

The Leader with Seven Faces

What you are
Awareness
Responsibility
Identity

"If I am not for myself, then who will be for me?
And if I am only for myself, then what am I?
And if not now, when?"[17]
The Ethics of the Fathers

"*What* are you?" is a rather direct, if not aggressive question. It is different from 'who are you?' 'What' implies what kind of material, what kind of individual, what kind of animal! And this is how the lines in Ethics of The Fathers, one of the Jewish religious books, read (see quote above).

It doesn't say 'who are you' or 'what kind of person'. It is a simple, straight forward, uncompromising 'what'! The lines have always impressed me. My knowledge of Jewish spirituality is close to zero, but when somebody told me about Rabbi Hillel's lines a long time ago, something clicked in my brain. This '*what* are you?' has followed me ever since.

---

[17] Rabbi Hillel, Ethics of the Fathers, 1:14

There is a sort of Quality Control division inside the leader's brain that asks all those questions such as '*what* are you?' And this is a good way to describe one of the seven faces of the leader. I'd like to explore three dimensions here:

- **Awareness.** How the leader acquires a sense of reality about himself and others. How conscious he is about strengths and limitations, both of himself and his environment.

- **Responsibility.** Responsibility and accountabilities get to the core of the 'what are you' question. For the leader, responsibility is both glory and burden.

- **Identity**. Another angle of the 'what' has to do with the ability of the leader to create a sense of belonging: for himself, his followers and the entire organization. Identity also has to do with answering the question 'where is home?' and, ultimately, 'what are you?'

Awareness

Much has been written about the need for any of us to know ourselves. The same applies to the leader. Conventional wisdom says that it's going to be difficult to understand others and lead the organization if one hasn't got a good handle of strengths and weaknesses in one's own backyard. At least the following dimensions are part of this awareness:

- Awareness of oneself
- Awareness of others
- Awareness of the organization and the environment

▶ Influence and power

I have alluded to this in more than one place in this book. The leader needs to be conscious of his power and influence. He needs to know what mechanisms are in place. It may be that it is his simple hierarchical authority which confers him the power and the influence. It may be that it is more the trust that he generates or his technical competencies. It may be a mixture of all this. But it is essential that the leader reflects upon these. Organizations are full of pavlovian reflexes that make people react to a position of authority. A client who has been in the military told me a story of a general who walked into a room and made the comment, *"This window could do with a lick of paint"*, said with the same enthusiasm and depth as *"what a nice weather today!"* The following day the room was painted.

I have seen a senior leader in a pharmaceutical R&D facility make a comment in the corridor about some type of clinical studies that should be put in place. The following week, at least two people were preparing documentation and budgets. The studies didn't make sense whatsoever, nor would anybody in an R&D facility acknowledge to you that the mechanism to initiate a multi-million dollar study was a passing comment by a mighty leader in the men's room. But, hey, I have seen it. These may be extreme and caricature cases, but day-to-day life in organizations contains a fair amount of reactivity to a leader's adrenaline. Leaders need to be aware of the relative dosage of influence, authority and execution power they have (for better or for worse!) without taking preliminary answers at face value!

▶ Emotional intelligence

In recent years, the term emotional intelligence (EI) has become popular in management. It has created a sub-industry of its own with consulting, coaching and training books. Conceptually, it is very simple. The 'old intelligence' based upon rationality is, well, old, the proponents say. We need to bring the emotional components to the party.

We use our emotions all the time. We like and dislike, things make us comfortable or uncomfortable, we get angry or pleased. All this is normal life. But a great deal of organizational life, particular hard core business life, has always had antibodies against emotions. Emotions are a dirty word. In the English language in particular, an emotional leader is not a good leader. I have mentioned this before. It is even close to being a dangerous one, because God knows what those emotions can do to fair judgment of things. Our cultural stereotype of a (business) leader includes being calm, rational, logical, and 'well-balanced', always able to distinguish facts from 'emotions' and keeping his brain cool all the time. Well, who can blame the cultural creators of the stereotype? If you lived through the Cold War, the last thing you wanted was an emotional world leader with an easy finger on the red button.

However, the surgical removal of emotions from the leader's life deprives him from humanity. Far from suppressing emotions, we need to spot them, embrace them, understand how they influence things and master them. As a consultant on leadership, I can spot maturity in a management team and good leadership skills - perhaps of the collective type - when people in the room can have a conversation or debate *with* emotions associated. *"Fred, my dear mighty leader, you seem to be passionate about A, but quite frankly, I think it's crap"*, followed by some degree of collective laughter. All that, versus collective nodding in the meeting room and ferociously whispering criticism during the coffee break with other colleagues. I very often play the card of my psychiatric training by saying to a group, *"come on, tell me how you feel, I need feelings, I am a psychiatrist!"* I want to make the point that it is OK to bring the 'feeling thing' to the table. Once the ice is broken, I usually get a very rich delivery of new angles, sentiments of uncertainty, fears, excitement, boredom or any other oil of the organizational machinery. We always gain from it.

Like anything else, these skills need to be learnt. Leaders need to facilitate an environment where it is safe to express emotions, where using them is an advantage and where rational discourse can be accompanied by feelings and beliefs without cross-disruption. Some leaders need extra help in this area and in those cases, coaching may be very useful. There are well tried pathways and methods.

▶ *360 degrees for all seasons*

Emotional and social intelligence are not things you install by doing a 360° feedback exercise! 360s have become very popular and standardized in some cultural environments, mainly the Anglo-Saxon one. Usually via a questionnaire, somebody 'neutral' gathers feedback on a particular person (the leader), perhaps about his qualities, perhaps behaviours, perhaps both. Although as a tool this may be useful, the idea that by feeding things back to the leader, he will become (a) 'aware', (b) 'master of his emotions' and (c) will put things in practice 'to change', is very naïve, to say the least! 360° feedback is a tool that needs to be used with a lot of professional care and in the context of a professional or personal development plan. When used in automatic pilot mode, it is useless and may be dangerous. I always surprise people, including my colleagues in the firm, by my apparent level of antibodies against 360s. My bias against them is threefold:

(1) I have seen them used as a weapon to castigate people, to single them out or even to humiliate them. Bob seems to have problems with his team; there is a lot of noise about what's going on in his department. Bob's boss and the HR guru decide that it is time for Bob to have a 360. "*Bob, look how much we care about you, we are investing in your development, have a 360, you'll need to talk to X consultant, he'll give you a call.*" Bob has the 360 done, which entails about a dozen people - including some direct reports - giving input 'in confidence'. So they do. And guess what, it's open season to crucify Bob. After all, if the company is doing this, there may be something wrong, so let's

amplify the weaknesses and, why not, all those annoying aspects of Bob's personality. Those of you who have a very different, positive experience of the 360 would not recognize themselves in this vignette. Fine. Congrats. But, believe me, this is happening every day in our organizations. Obviously, a way to minimize the risk of singling somebody out, creating 'a special case', is to have the 360-practice normalized as part of regular 'routine. Yes, agreed, that's much better.

(2) Bob's boss and the head of HR may be using 'the tool' as a way to avoid direct dialog with Bob, in order to understand and possibly help. They are abdicating their responsibilities as leaders and relying on a process hidden under the attractiveness and cleanness of confidentiality to address what should be addressed across the table over a cappuccino. Maybe they are just practicing power gymnastics. Maybe. Again, if you are saying that many people are involved in the process, then it is a bit different because it helps with data gathering of some scale. But the concern stands.

(3) In many cases, the end of the feedback is the end of the story, so the Bobs of the day are left with a list of things that 'need improvement' and no mechanism to improve them with.

Bombarding people with personal data (personality tests, 360, skills and competences assessment) is no guarantee for personal growth and behavioural change. Emotional intelligence is not just 'created' by the feedback but by the ability of the individual to integrate the emotions, mature on them and try to master them. There have to be (organizational) mechanisms in place to do that, otherwise it is like a medical diagnosis with no treatment associated.

► *Working preferences and styles*

There is an extremely useful method to gain professional awareness and at the same time create shared understanding amongst a group of people, perhaps a management team. It has to do with understanding your own working preferences and styles. There are many tools that people use, amongst them the well established Meyers Briggs assessment. The problem with some 'personality type' assessments is that they have a hell of an assumption embedded. Indeed, your personality is supposed to be stable across the board, no matter in what situation you are. That includes work, taking the kids to sports, helping in the church, regular family life, going with friends and volunteering at the local community centre. But there is a substantial amount of data that shows that how we 'work at work' differs from other situations. Assessment tools that are 'work-based' have a clear advantage. They are also more 'neutral' and tend to create less anxiety in people who don't like the idea of 'personality tests'. The ones we use are based on the assessment of four dimensions that differentiate each of us from others:

- **The way we use information.** Some people are very analytical; others are able to use the information in a more 'creative' way.

- **The way we make decisions**. Some people are more comfortable making decisions based on data, other people seem to be prone to make them based upon 'beliefs'.

■ **The way we organize things.** Some people prefer a flexible way, others a more structured one.

■ **The way we relate to others** *in the workplace.* Some people cook things up by themselves in an 'introvert' manner, other people need 'a meeting' or 'a group' to move forward.

There are obviously more dimensions that differentiate human beings in the workplace, but these four are simple and rather universal. When the individual data is shared in the group, many 'ahas!' tend to occur. Many so-called 'communication problems' or 'team difficulties' simply come from the fact that people tend to work in their preferred 'zones of comfort'. Once these have been clarified, it is easier to understand some irritations, dysfunctions and bottlenecks.

These kinds of dimensions are the A, B, C of understanding team dynamics. Management teams that go through this kind of exercise tend to create a new baseline for the team faster, which allows it to progress to higher levels of effectiveness and leadership. As a leader, you need to create some mechanisms for your teams to become aware of themselves, those dimensions or others. I consider this 'A,B'C' so important, that I try to go through this exercise as a baseline as much as possible, even if my consulting assignment is not directly related to the topic of leadership. To inject some leadership understanding of the 'map of the team' (in terms of working preferences) has always paid off for me, no matter what.

▶ Social intelligence

Social intelligence is a complement of the emotional intelligence. Often this term is used as a synonym for social skills or ability to interact with others in a rich way and use those relationships as an asset. In practical terms, leaders need to be aware of the dynamics in the organization. Put simply, they need to be close to it. It has to do with understanding the sources of conflict, the bottlenecks, the day-to-day frictions, the mechanisms of power, etc. In all those things, there is always a mixture of reality and fiction. And navigating through them to try to distinguish between them, is not always easy. From all the aspects of this organizational awareness and closeness to-what's-going-on, I'd like to suggest these key areas:

- Understanding the real-life motivational mechanisms inside the organization you lead.
- Flagging *dysfunctionality* or deterioration.

▶ Why are you still here?

Exit interviews are common practice in many organizations today. When somebody leaves, he or she is interviewed, perhaps by the HR department, to understand the reasons and hopefully to learn one or two lessons. It sounds like a good idea. Two problems, however: timing and independence. Both are linked. If the interview is carried out in the heat of the resignation, it may be contaminated by the emotions. What people say at that time and what they may say a month later, may be a bit different. It is also natural to expect that what one says to the HR manager of the company and what one could say to a third party independent interviewer, is also different.

In many cases I know, however, exit interviews look more like a case of ticking some boxes by the HR department and recording something for the file for the sake of doing it, rather than a genuine attempt to understand why people leave the organization. Genuine is the key word. It is well-documented that the list of reasons given is not necessarily the 'right list' when a more thorough investigation takes place or when independent studies are done. Consistently over the years, the key reasons for leaving - when examined independently and in the cold - are related to people's direct management: I can't stand him anymore, management doesn't care, not getting along well, and combinations thereof. There are, of course, many others but these ones have proven consistent in research. The official lines given at the time of leaving, however, are more along the lines of: *"time to move on"*, *"better offer, better salary"*, *"promotion to higher position"*, etc. All of which may be true as well. But the timing of the exit may have also been triggered by a deteriorating interface with managers or 'the system'.

The moment when people in managerial roles start answering calls from head-hunters, may be determined by a combination of factors, but research suggests that the immediate management structure and dynamics and quality of leadership is one that has a lot to do with it. Of course, it would be silly to generalizes, but silly as well to ignore these consistent findings.

In many organizations, these subtle problems of interpretations do not exist. They simply do not carry out formal exit interviews of any sort! I mentioned before in this book that when a laptop disappears from the office, you launch an investigation, but when a multi-thousand dollar employee leaves, we say 'that's life'. It is perhaps more convenient to ignore the evidence and rely on assumptions. Assumptions are a great management weapon.

There is another side to the exit interviews coin. They are sometimes called 'stay interviews' and are practiced by a fraction of companies. The idea is also very simple: ask people why they haven't left. Don't wait until they do; ask people why they are still there and why they have 'decided' to stay. The question of independence, again, seems an obvious one. Stay interviews are a great form to investigate motivation mechanisms in the organization. Why people stay is equal to what motivates them. Unlike exit interviews - which are time-dependent and are determined by when the individual says goodbye - stay interviews can be built-in as a constant process of obtaining random samples. They should be happening all the time at the right dose to be able to build good evidence.

Many organizations use once a year surveys called 'employee satisfaction' or 'attitude' surveys. There is, of course, a connection between these concepts and proper stay interviews, but just that: a connection. Even if the practice of those once a year surveys is established, the issue, believe it or not, is often one of what to make of the data. Why? Because you sometimes get back a massive dossier of multicolour graphs, the interpretation of which is far from straight forward. However, those multicolour bars will immediately prompt management to make judgements under the comfort of 'presence of hard data'. Some leaders are very good at ascribing causality to data. *"Of course people say so and so. We knew that, the survey was done three months ago and that was at the peak of when we were dealing with problem X. Of course people complain of such and such, there is a culture here of stressing Y and Z."* Give me some data and I will create the script.

The topic of the value and use of those types of surveys would require a very big space. Let's just say that they may be useful tools in the context of a broader understanding of what's going on, but that they carry a high dose of risk if they are not used properly. Am I saying anything new or different from any other assessment tool? Perhaps not, but I have seen many employee satisfaction and attitude surveys being used to trigger many reactions ranging from complacency to specific HR remedial policies that try to 'address' the issue and often do so in isolation from a broader organizational strategy. OK, this is for another day.

Independent stay interviews have the following benefits:

1. Building a database of the truth! Some leaders seem to believe that they know what's going on in the organization but the real picture is often different. Why people are part of your team may be because of the sexy science and technology around or because it pays the mortgage or because they live next door and it is convenient. Of course, it may be, and probably is, a combination of these. But surely you would like to know what mechanism plays what, just in case the main reason is the short driving distance from home. So when you decide to move offices, the sexy pipeline and the privilege of working for you put together, don't get even near to compensating for the proposed new geography. The market is suddenly flooded with your best unconditional admirers!

In these interviews, one can ask not only why you are still there but also what would trigger you not be there anymore. That may reveal black spots and serve as warning signals. The key of these techniques is in the word 'building', that is, something that is not a one-off shot in time, like the attitude and satisfaction surveys tend to be. Progressively, some patterns of reasons and connections will emerge. By doing it on an ongoing basis, you dismiss the risk of the immediate interpretation and the rushed policy decisions. From time to time, leadership teams would be asked to confront the data and discuss, to see the connections between things and to understand 'the real organization' that is underneath. Surprises and unexpected answers would then be less threatening and people would be less prone to a rapid, often half-baked action.

2. Map the behavioural DNA of the organization. Stay interviews will uncover behaviours that are common in the organization, that are acceptable or unacceptable. They will show 'patterns of doing things'. This is again one of the areas where leader's assumptions are sometimes further away from reality. The organization may have declared values and beliefs, for example, around teamwork and collaboration. 'The system' - that is leadership plus staff plus processes, etc - may feel comfortable thinking that these are present (after all, they have been declared) and indeed you may have a few examples of this happening. It is not until a proper behavioural audit takes place - and stay interviews are a good vehicle for that - that the assumptions may be validated. It may be that the examples of good teamwork that are showcased are the only ones existing, whilst the organization on the whole suffers from lack of collaboration between people outside these examples. Perhaps it is the other way around: people feel good about staying in an organization where teamwork is widespread and that may be a real mechanism of retention. You'd better know this and use it.

3. Find out about real rewards. One of the problems with reward and compensation systems is that it is usually very biased, if not totally biased, towards money. The only possible sophistication of a money-based incentive programme is more money. Money is part of the reward system but, as everybody knows, only part. In fact, in any organization, there is always a wealth of reward mechanisms, only a fraction of which are used. Many forms of individual or team recognition - such as time spend with the manager, recognition of small achievements, work flexibility, you name them - the list of things that have the potential of reinforcing the stay of an individual is huge. But it is also hidden. Until you start asking the question, of course.

If you really want to know what motivates people (what makes them stay), I suggest a terribly unsophisticated technique: go and ask them. And this is what stay interviews can do, because you will find the answers even before you have asked the question. Conventional management practices tend to create universal systems of reward and recognition, all full of assumptions such as 'shares and stock options are good for you'. One of the main assumptions that needs to be debunked - and this is an easy one because there is plenty of data around - is that employee ownership leads to better company performance. This is simply not true, but we keep assuming that it is and we keep generating more and more share ownership schemes of more (or less) complexity.

4. Discover the tyranny of small things. It is not until you actively try to find out that people discover how apparently 'small things' (some cumbersome processes, small difficulties, imperfection of systems, inadequate response after request for help, etc) are in reality big things that have the potential of making the stay unpleasant. You may want to install a sophisticated information management system in a research department and, following the customer-driven mantra, you will ask your 'internal customers' what exactly they want. Proud of this customer-centric-service-oriented action, the CIO may dictate to carry out a survey of 'needs' and 'requirements'. Expecting to get back requests for capabilities to do sophisticated data mining, state of the art social network analysis and real-time collaborative spaces that can connect synchronically (!), what you get is, *"could you please fix the emails, they are slow and a pain, and, by the way, the new keyboards are cheap and noisy."* Normal people in normal daily life have many, say, mundane needs, and the fulfilment or non-fulfilment of these can create tipping points in their motivation.

In my own practice, I prefer to call this exercise 'Organizational check-up' instead of stay interviews, but the fundamentals are the same. It is impossible to substitute the active finding out of what's going on in the organization with anything better than asking people directly or indirectly and building subsequent maps of connections. Investing in this is fundamental in order to have a clear picture of what retains or doesn't retain people around you.

Many years ago, somebody asked the then most prominent Spanish professor of Medicine, what the best technological piece of equipment or technological breakthrough was, required to practice modern medicine. Gregorio Marañon responded, *"the chair"*. Sitting next to a patient and listening was worth more to him than anything else. In leadership, we still need to discover 'the chair', that is, asking people and talking with them. And any leader has the budget to do that.

▶ *Spotting organizational broken windows and graffiti*

The benefit of asking questions such as 'why are you still here?', is that it gives the leader a great deal of the organizational awareness that he needs, and therefore provides good material for both therapy and prevention. A second component of this comes from spotting potential early, perhaps subtle signs of organizational deterioration. Leaders with good social skills would be very sensitive to the principles and examples that will follow.

Let me go back a few years. James Wilson and George Kelling probably didn't expect to trigger a massive policy movement of colossal socio-political consequences when they wrote an article in *The Atlantic Monthly* in 1982 entitled *Broken Windows: The Police and Neighbourhood Safety*. The authors dealt with observations of a well-known sequence of events in some urban communities that were summarized like this:

"Evidence of decay (accumulated trash, broken windows, deteriorated building exteriors) remains in the neighbourhood for a reasonably long period of time. People who live and

work in the area feel more vulnerable and begin to withdraw. They become less willing to intervene to maintain public order (for example, to attempt to break up groups of rowdy teens loitering on street corners) or to address physical signs of deterioration. Sensing this, teens and other possible offenders become bolder and intensify their harassment and vandalism. Residents become yet more fearful and withdraw further from community involvement and upkeep. Some people leave if they can. This atmosphere then attracts offenders from outside the area, who sense that it has become a vulnerable and less risky site for crime."

Following the publication, two things happened. First of all, a full theory emerged from what had only been an observation of reality, one too familiar for many of our cities today. Second, actions were taken in many places in the US, and some of them were counterintuitive, misinterpreted or controversial even to this day. The glue that explains it all belongs to the behavioural and social sciences. I suggest that the theory is extremely useful beyond the unpleasantness of some suburban life to understand organizational decline in our safer and perhaps even cosier organizations. As in suburban US, there are practical ways to deal with the organizational deterioration, or, alternatively, dare I say, get out before it's too late.

The 'Broken windows theory' suggests that relatively small - and in itself often harmless - realities (broken windows, graffiti on walls, litter on the streets, etc.) have the power, if not addressed promptly, of creating big social changes by sending dangerous signals to the environment. These signals are interpreted as *"nobody cares much around here, it is safe to break things, litter or vandalize, etc"*, which makes the place attractive for people who engage in those kinds of behaviours and triggers further disorders.

Prolonged harmless graffiti leads to more broken windows and wider vandalism because it acts as a signal for *"you can get away with destruction here"* which opens the door to broad disorder. To put it bluntly, small deterioration can create irreversible decline. The theory would become a pillar for what years later would be known as the 'zero tolerance' law enforcement policy in places such as New York, which has often been misunderstood, I suspect even by many of its implementers.

The conventional wisdom of the action to be taken to fix these problems would read: *"don't let them get away with it, punish them"*. But in behavioural sciences terms, punishment has very moderate effects, at least if compared with what we call 'extinction', that is, making sure that if there were incentives for those engaged in the disorder, these would no longer be available.

In behavioural sciences, we call behavioural reinforcement anything that has the ability to increase the probability of a given behaviour. For the New Yorker gangs engaged in massive graffiti on the trains on the underground service, for example, the reinforcement could probably be understood in terms of sense of power, by seeing the effects of their actions all over the place and the apparent immunity they enjoyed. Power, ego busting, sense of achievement, group spirit, whatever it is or was, is reinforcing those behaviours: that is, is motivating these people to do it again.

Whilst conventional wisdom and popular psychology would have suggested that the police should find and punish those perpetrators, a truly behavioural sciences based approach would favour the unavailability of the reward over the application of the punishment. And this is precisely what people in places such as New York did. Instead of 'find them and punish them' they opted for 'find them and show them the futility of their actions'. How? By cleaning the graffiti as fast as they could, in some cases in front of the perpetrator's own noses. And overall crime declined.

The 'Broken windows' policy has clear consequences, as a commentator in the *Washington Post* described:

"The theory has spawned a revolution in law enforcement and neighbourhood activism. Broken windows? Get building owners to replace them. Graffiti on the walls? Scrub them clean, then get tough with graffiti artists. Abandoned cars? Haul them away. Drunks on the sidewalks? Get them off the streets, too.

Or as an official American neighbourhood website dictates:

"These 'order strategies' such as those listed below help to deter and reduce crime. Quick replacement of broken windows; prompt removal of abandoned vehicles: fast clean-up of illegally dumped items, litter and spilled garbage; quick paint out of graffiti; finding (or building) better places for teens to gather than street corners; fresh paint on buildings and clean sidewalks and street gutters".

The 'Broken windows' model is powerful and attractive and, as such, it is not surprising that by using it to explain lots of things, it has accumulated its own critics. For example, the significant decline in crime in many US cities over the period of 'zero tolerance implementation' is portrayed by some as a consequence of the policy, whilst others see it as a simple accentuation of a trend that was already present and linked to many other social factors. A more recent theory of crime decline is found in the controversial thesis *The Impact of Legalized Abortion on Crime*, written in 2001 by Stanford University law professor John Donohue and University of Chicago Economics professor Steven Levitt. This paper explained the drop in crime in the USA over the years USA as a consequence of the implementation of legalized abortion. Levitt put it simply to the *New York Times*: "*A difficult home environment leads to an increased risk of criminal activity. Increased abortion reduced unwantedness and therefore lower[ed] criminal activity.*"

The complexity of any 'explanation' in the social sciences is enormous and therefore not unexpectedly contentious. Cause and effect in social sciences is a tricky affair. But the 'broken windows' model is one that can help us to understand and deal with situations in day-to-day leadership in our business organizations. And this is a conversation worth having here.

We have our own versions of graffiti and litter in our companies, and I am not talking about the cleanliness of the toilets. Organizational life is full of rules of the game: some of them explicit, others tacit; some necessary, some not; some enabling us to do our jobs, some plain silly or only created to satisfy big egos. In non-judgemental behavioural terms, rules create the borders of what is acceptable and what's not - whether good or bad - and therefore serve as a map for people in the organization. If the rule is stupid, people should be able to challenge it by trying to change it, but never by simply ignoring it.

There is a trick here. Ignoring a stupid rule because of your conviction of its uselessness - and being able to do so without being penalized - may have the intended good consequence of making that rule less stable, which is good news! Isn't that what you would like to see after all? However, being visible in the organization (for example, at some level of leadership and authority) and ignoring the rule (for the same reasons of conviction), is a graffiti signal to others saying: rules are not really taken seriously here. This may be unintended, but potentially it could be a powerful trigger for widespread lack of compliance. In the process of fixing A (by ignoring it), we have created problem B. Also, many rules are not stupid: they simply guide efficacy or effectiveness or time management or information flow or quality maintenance.

If you see an increased lack of compliance, a progressive rise in loose ends, unfinished discussions, decisions half-baked, delayed implementations, poor usage of an information management system or agreed actions not taking place, and people are getting away with it all, you may be seeing broken windows. As in the social theory described, these facts in isolation may not be big enough to expect a breakdown of the firm from them, but - whether you wanted it or not - they generate a multiplying effect with possibly unintended consequences. You may think that this is simply a lack of discipline, and you may be right, but this is unfortunately just a label that means very little in behavioural terms. The reality is, that if there is no negative consequence (for the perpetrators) and if the behaviours are self-reinforced (by the fact that loose compliance, for example, is simply possible), the place will attract other non-compliance realities of bigger magnitude before you know it. You may also perhaps call it poor leadership, period. In which case, you may be right as well in saying that leadership is more unlikely to see anything particularly wrong.

I am more interested - and I am trying to get you interested (!) - in the utility of 'broken windows signals'. That is, symptoms that the leader may have spotted and that - although not necessarily an expression of a true and full 'broken windows environment' - should alert him early enough and ask him to make a judgment on whether behind those symptoms there is something more serious going on.

The more those loose ends appear with some sort of tendency to increase, the more you as a leader should be alerted. Together with the examples given above, watch out for meeting minutes that suddenly disappear from the agenda and don't seem to be reviewed anymore, requests for issue input followed by progressive silence, deadlines that appear more 'flexible' than ever (or are simply not met), circulated briefing documents that nobody really read, sudden loss of clarity of who is accountable for what, perhaps with an increase in so-called 'shared responsibility', requested formats (for meetings, reports, input sought) that are ignored or repeated postponement of events due to lack of quorum.

All those are 'broken windows' in the management system. They may not kill the firm by themselves, but they may be symptoms of an underlying pathology. In the best case, there may not be death on the horizon, but the firm's weak immunological system will simply attract other infections.

A worse case is when all these things seem to be 'new' or were non-existing in a previous history of the organization. What it means is that the firm has a temperature and the fever should alert you. And alert is a good word. Whilst very poor organizational performance may be shocking enough to shock the system and trigger immediate remedial measures, a softer increased tolerance for marginal performance is always a sign of serious deterioration that can be easily overlooked. It is the equivalent of walking through the same street every day and not noticing the broken windows and the graffiti.

You may decide that this is all very well, but that it's not happening or not possible in your organization. After all, you are not one of those companies! For the most optimistic, I would like to remind you of a social experiment which Philip Zimbardo, Professor Emeritus of psychology at Stanford University (who we also encountered in previous pages), conducted in 1969. This is considered an old precursor to 'broken windows' and you'll see why. Zimbardo left two identical 'vulnerable' cars on the street in two different places and waited for them to be vandalized. The one left in the Bronx in New York was stripped bare in a day. The one left on the street in Palo Alto, California, remained untouched for a week. After a week, Zimbardo himself put a hammer through one of the windows and, as a report put it, *"as though this act and its impunity were the starting gun they were waiting for, the Californians rallied round to destroy that car just as thoroughly"*. All it takes is a broken window in your organization. You as leader should not take it lightly.

▶ *Awareness of the seven faces*

All the themes, dimensions and topics mapped for the Seven Faces require awareness from the leader. In each of the chapters I have referred to this, although with different emphasis. The promenade now will be simple:

- Awareness of your language, the 'translation' and 'articulation' of a strategy (your strategy?), for example, and the creation of meaning for the organization.

- Awareness of the maps that you make available to others, the destinations described, the journeys ahead and whether people following have an understanding of all of them.

- Awareness of what kind of organization is built every day under your leadership, what kind of 'spaces' and what kind of homes (for talent, for relationships, etc). Awareness of your legacy.

- Awareness of the values and beliefs, not just at personal level but also at the collective level. Awareness of what you have declared 'non-negotiable'.

- Awareness of what's driving you as a leader and what people see as driving you! Awareness of the styles of leading, for you and for others, and the degrees of *freedom* in the structure of your organization.

- Awareness of your responsibilities and of the identities that you create or simply allow to coexist (as we will see below).

- Awareness of the kind of role modelling that you are exercising and its consequences. Awareness of your capacity as leader to create change.

Responsibility

The English language provides an intriguing distinction between accountability and responsibility. Not so in other languages. Responsibility is translated as *responsabilité* in French, *responsabilidad* in Spanish and *responsabilità* in Italian. Accountability is translated into…the same: *responsabilité, responsabilidad, responsabilità.* However, the word roots are different. Accountability has to do with accounting, counting, taking into account, give account of, etc. Responsibility has to do with responding or to respond.

I use the distinction to suggest to clients that it seems as if *many* people could respond to things, but that it would be useful if only *one* counts! In other words, you can share responsibility, but not accountability. That clarifies where the buck stops!

One of the modern cancers in modern organizational life is the absolute mess in accountabilities that is often seen in companies. The matrix systems, the multidisciplinary project teams and the over-inclusiveness culture (that requires twenty representatives or 'stakeholders' in the room, even if the stake is doubtful and they are not holding much) have created a system of blurred responsibilities as foggy as an early winter morning in England.

There is an underlying assumption, for example, that 'sharing' decision-making is good for empowerment, motivation and the rest. This assumption is flawed. Sharing the *process* of decision-making may be productive and very possibly motivating. Sharing the *decision* itself is bad management. Similarly, 'the team' does not make decisions. People (in teams or not in teams) do.

As leader, you should be careful to allocate responsibilities (shared or not) and accountabilities (not shared). You have to be very clear on what exactly you are accountable for. The same for members of your team. An organization with clarity in responsibilities and accountabilities has the organizational advantage.

▶ You may choose not to be a leader!

Also, as leader, be careful what you choose to be accountable for. You'll be 'on your own' and you'll have to stick to it. Incidentally, you may choose not to be a leader. I tease my clients with this assertion, which - to tell you the truth - is not as flipping mad as it sounds. Many people (though not all) in leadership positions reach those positions through career progression that takes them to report to the chairman, or the CEO, or a senior person. They become leaders-by-default, by virtue of the organization chart. And indeed, that may be what they want. Great. But they do not need to be there. They could choose not to be there. They could choose not to be part of that leadership team, for example. Strictly speaking, this is always true. I know, I know, you don't go around requesting demotions but, again, strictly speaking, nobody has forced them to 'be there'! But, if you choose to be there, my friend, well, it's a package deal. It comes with higher bonuses and usually larger accountabilities, including the welfare of a few hundred (or thousand) human beings and their pension funds.

There is a test for leadership. I am not talking about the (collective) five that I am proposing in the epilogue of this book. It is a mirror test, and reads as follows:

> *When you get what you want in your struggle for self*
> *And the world makes you king for a day,*
> *Just go to a mirror and look at yourself,*
> *And see what that man has to say.*
>
> *For it isn't your father or mother or wife,*
> *Who judgment upon you must pass;*
> *The fellow whose verdict counts most in your life*
> *Is the one staring back from the glass.*
>
> *He's the fellow to please, never mind all the rest.*
> *For he's with you clear up to the end,*
> *And you've passed the most dangerous, difficult test*
> *If the man in the glass is your friend.*
>
> *You may be like Jack Horner and 'chisel' a plum,*
> *And think you're a wonderful guy,*
> *But the man in the glass says you're only a bum*
> *If you can't look him straight in the eye.*

*You may fool the whole world down the pathway of
years.
And get pats on the back as you pass,
But your final reward will be the heartaches and tears
If you've cheated the man in the glass.*

This is Dale Wimbrow's poem *Man in the Glass* (1934),
which elevated the mirror to the category of management tool.

Identity

This is '*what* are you' at its best. Leadership has a tremendous
ability to create a 'sense of belonging', to create 'homes'. It
may be the company, an idea, a project, a concept of a future,
a vision. It is often by default that this happens, but good
leaders will make the process conscious for themselves and
others.

Sense of belonging is a tricky one. In the era of mergers,
acquisitions, ephemeral enterprises and 'change of control' as
a way of life, it is hard to root. Traditional thinking always
linked loyalty and belonging. When today people are asked to
belong to a moving target, it also makes it harder for loyalty.

It has always fascinated me how people respond to the
question: "*what are you doing or what do you do for a
living?*" In caricature terms and in informal conversations
(using distorted English-speak!), many people used to
respond: "*I am IBM, or I am GE or I am GM, or I am Merck*".
Or its variant, "*I am at Merck*, etc", only to be followed by, "*I
am* in *marketing*", to be followed by, perhaps, "*I deal with*

international products". The language and order has always been a good expression of 'belonging'. In that example, the pecking order is company → function → doing for real.

Some professions have always been a bit of an exception: "*I am a medical doctor, I am at Merck*", the medical tribe would usually come first. Some other tribes have gained front row status: "*I am IT, I work for so and so*", giving up-front signs of the attachment to a supposed universal set of skills and competencies. It sounds in those examples as if a doctor is always a doctor first (whether he is working for a pharmaceutical company or not) and an IT professional is IT first. They seem to say that they belong to some sort of race and then have joined something called 'a company'. Watching people describing their affiliations is to me a semi-anthropological exercise that tells me a lot about belonging and loyalty.

There is nothing like the Irish who always call 'home' anywhere between Sligo and Cork, Belfast and Galway, or Dublin and Connemara, no matter how many million miles away they are, or indeed, whether they have been on that small island for anything but a fraction of their life. 'Going home' for an Irishman (or Irishwoman) is never going to the house where they sleep every day. There is only one 'home', and it usually takes a ferry or an airplane to get there. It is perhaps hidden somewhere in the Celtic universal-archetypes-big-cupboard because Celtic history, traditions and spirituality have 'places' at a sacred level. The Irish know where they belong!

People in organizations today would have a little more trouble to define 'home'. I am neither suggesting there is something romantic in the manager's identification with a company, nor

What you are

I do think that 'belonging' and 'loyalty' are straight forward mechanisms. But, one way or another, all of us want to belong somewhere. Historically, organizations used to provide those 'home' effects. It is harder now. Although business life is somehow more transitional now, the leader needs to create a sense of belonging and attachment to - if not the company - the team, the project, the collective future or the commonality of interests of his people. It is not necessarily about a single identity (for all people) but to allow for identities to flourish.

On a personal basis, the leader often plays a particular character. He is there as inspirational force, as a saviour, as a man of destiny, as a technical authority, a general, a driver (of change), etc. And he is often stuck with the identity associated with a particular historical role. He may not like some of those characters, but they may just come with the job! As a leader, reflecting upon identity - both at a personal level and with the organization in mind - is not a trivial thing. Organizations today look more like hosts of multiple identities and belongings. And it is perhaps in the hosting itself, its quality and its breadth, that the best skills are needed.

Let me summarize by saying that all the topics created around leader's awareness - of himself, of the organization, of his responsibilities, of the identity and belonging - require the development of emotional and social intelligence. This is not a simple exercise. It needs - guess what? - practise!

A good way to start is to refine 'one's senses' by learning how to have a good grasp of the organization. And understanding that many need equal emphasis on the extraordinary life (crisis, peaks of activity) as well as on the ordinary life, the routine, 'the obvious'. Instead of expanding on the latter, let me finish with a little tale.

A man was leading a caravan of donkeys and crossing the border almost every day, coming back with apparently the same caravan. Each donkey carried two bags of sand, one at each side. The border guard got progressively intrigued and suspected that the man was smuggling something, hidden in those bags. Very often he would stop the man with the caravan and would search the bags, only to find sand and more sand. Over the years, this practice continued and the border guard could never find anything in those bags. One day, the border guard retired. Once he had retired, he went back to the border and saw the man with the same caravan. *"Look, I am not in a position of authority anymore. I have been watching you, stopping you and searching your bags. I have found nothing. But I am still convinced that you are smuggling something. Would you tell me now? What are you smuggling?"* To which the man answered: *"donkeys"*.

Questions

In the leader's own development, nothing will substitute the need for closeness to the organization. The answers to many questions are often in front of you: in your own people, in your own organization. Keep your eyes open! The 'what you are' is at the core of leadership.

- Use the list to trigger new questions or to attempt to answer them! Make notes, use the book!
- Commit to one single step to 'answer the question'. These steps may look like actions you want to take, questions you want to ask other people in your organization or 'practice' that you want to do at your next opportunity.

Awareness

- Dou you have a clear idea/have you reflected upon your level of influence and power?
- Would you describe yourself as 'emotionally intelligent'?
- How 'free' is your team in terms of expressing emotions to you?
- How emotionally 'mature' is the organization below you?
- Do you use feedback systems such as the 360? Do you take care that they are used appropriately?
- How aware of your own 'areas of (working) preferences' are you?
- Have you reflected/do you have some hard data on how, for example, you make decisions, or how you would like to make them?

- How do you use information?
- How flexible or structured do you like your own environment to be?
- What are the implications of the above for you as leader in dealing with others and the organization?

Responsibility

- How aware are you as a leader of your own seven faces?
  - What you say?
  - Where you go?
  - What you build?
  - What you care about?
  - How you do it?
  - What you are?
  - What you do?
- Are you clear on your responsibilities and accountability?
- Do you make it clear to others?
- Are you a leader by virtue of some organization chart, by design, by accident, by 'progression'? Have you thought of the implications?

Identity

- Do you provide an identity and sense of belonging for your people? Could you answer it for yourself?
- If people working with you were asked about where they belong (in work terms), would you be surprised by the answers? Could you predict what they would say?
- What are the implications?

ACTION MAP
(some first pass questions)

Me   **My organization**

Me

Questions:
What's my own assessment of my emotional and social intelligence? Am I clear about my accountabilities as leader?

Questions:
Do I foster emotional intelligence in followers and in the organization? Do I nurture a sense of belonging? Identity? Identities?

My organization

Questions:
How would the organization/people around me see me in terms of the role that my emotions play? Of what I consider my accountabilities?

Questions:
Are we an emotional intelligent organization? Group? What's the identity of this place? How can we create a sense of belonging? Change?

This is a very simple set of questions to get you started
In your reflections and actions. Use the blank pages to
record your own questions and notes

▶ *Your Questions and Notes:*

What you are

► *Your Questions and Notes:*

The Leader with Seven Faces

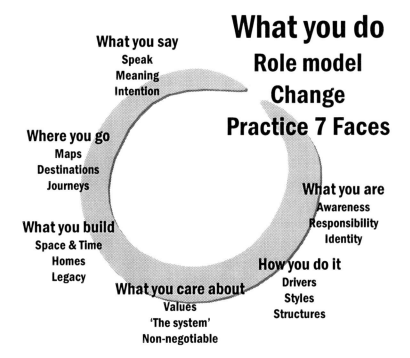

What you say
Speak
Meaning
Intention

What you do
Role model
Change
Practice 7 Faces

Where you go
Maps
Destinations
Journeys

What you are
Awareness
Responsibility
Identity

What you build
Space & Time
Homes
Legacy

How you do it
Drivers
Styles
Structures

What you care about
Values
'The system'
Non-negotiable

The Leader with Seven Faces

7

What you do
Role models
Change
Practicing seven faces

"If you don't like change,
you're going to like irrelevance even less"
General Eric Shinseki, former US Army Chief of Staff

You could say that 'what leaders do' is what really matters. That this is *the* chapter, or indeed *the* book. After all, 'saying', 'building' or 'going places' are forms of 'doing'. And you would be right. But I'd like to take this 'what you do' face of the leader to a higher level that somehow encompasses all 'doing'. And I'd like to offer two key dimensions for reflection: role modelling and driving change. Then I will add a third as a 'summary-of-summaries' (!) saying that what leaders should do is … practice the seven faces. So, let's go:

- **Role models.** Whether the leader wants it or not, he is a role model to others. The power of imitation is strong. The conscious use of role modelling powerful.

- **Change.** Leaders are drivers of change. So much is written about this that perhaps it may even be a turn-off for you. But change is not only inevitable, but also

269

desirable. The question is: what kind of change and how it is done. Leaders are 'change doers' in this face.

- **Practicing the Seven Faces**. You may remember the overriding philosophy of this book expressed in the early pages: leadership is not a theoretical concept; it is a practitioner's activity. Instead of spending a lot of energy debating if leadership is nature or nurture, we could use that energy 'practicing'. Perhaps we would then have more and better leaders!

Role models

I don't know whether you have ever reflected upon the power of imitation in general and in corporate cultures in particular. The higher the position of leadership, the more likely that people may mirror it one way or another. I was involved years ago in a situation where a new CEO came in and naturally started to find his way around over the first days and weeks. He could not have been more different from the previous one who had just retired. Let's call them Bill and John. Bill, the retired one, used to have very regular one-on-one meetings with his direct reports, monthly management team meetings and other more informal ones with subgroups of his close circle. Emails were very rare; he was not the electronic age type. Then John came in, fresh from the outside, He emailed profusely and did not organize one-on-ones, his philosophy being; "*when I need something from somebody (his direct reports) I'll walk in and if they need something, they should do the same; in the meantime we communicate by email*". It was his philosophy but he never articulated it, he just did things that way! Over the next weeks, the overall email traffic up to three levels down increased by 50% and many one-one-ones up to three levels down faded or disappeared. It was as if the organization shouted: *"John likes emails, emails are good, John doesn't like one-one-ones, one-on-ones are bad"*. John never said so. Indeed, John was asked later on about it and was stunned. He never intended to dictate a policy. He was just doing what worked best for him!

Over the years, I have come across different versions of the same pattern again and again. I am talking about leadership levels populated by engineers, PhDs, and other people whose brain activity is assumed to be quite healthy, but who start exhibiting 'conformity' as soon as signals from the 10th floor are sent down. As social animals, we all perform conformity all the time: as a way to belong to a group or not to feel dissociated with it. The way we dress is usually a good signal. We often adapt to the environment unconsciously. However, leadership behaviours may just trigger a cascade effect of signals, flooding conformity down across the levels.

And there are two sides to it. On the 'negative' side, you get cascade effects as the one described above. I am not even sure if the word 'negative' is appropriate, because it may be that John's system does work better! But I am referring to the automatic-pilot-non-thinking effect. On the 'positive' side, you could reflect upon this power of influence that you may have and use it to the advantage of your leadership and the organization. Don't underestimate the visibility of what you do, which - for better or for worse - is going to trigger some reactions, and reactions to reactions, and could very soon become the norm. If this is so, you have an obligation to be very aware of these mechanisms and their consequences.

▶ *A matter of trust*

What leaders do is very closely related to the amount of trust that is generated around them. Trust is a funny thing. It's also a delicate one. It often takes a while to create it, but it takes very little to destroy it. It's fragile and powerful at the same time. It is an important phenomenon from a psychological perspective because it represents a typical combination of the ways of working of our two brains: the old reptilian emotional one and the newest evolutionary rational one. As always with us humans, we are pulled in these two directions - rational and emotional - all the time.

The emotional part of trust has to do with what has been defined as 'exposing your vulnerabilities to people, but believing they will not take advantage of your openness'. In other words, I feel that I am safe (with somebody, with the group, with the company, with you as my leader), so it's OK to be open, sincere or ingenuous and it's not going to backfire. Translation: Leader, I trust you. It is our emotional brain at its best. You *feel* the trust between the two parts. If asked about the logic, you may just say, "*I don't know, I just trust him or her*".

There is however a second component, a rational one, where - as the experts say - "*you have assessed the probabilities of gain and loss, calculated expected utility based on hard performance data, and concluded that the person in question will behave in a predictable manner*". It sounds a bit cold, but that's probably because it is! Translation: I have figured out the pros and cons and decided that, on balance, I can trust you as a leader. It is my rationality that takes me there, my risk assessment with my rational brain in the driver's seat.

Although the scholars insist on the two aspects, there is little doubt that most of the time we work in emotional-trust mode. And this is perhaps why trust is so fragile.

There are reams of analysis on trust. Psychology, psycho-sociology, sociology, anthropology, politics and modern behavioural economics all address the question of trust one way or another. Business management adopts it and organizational development incorporates it heavily. The latter people will tell you that trust is the real oil of the organization: it makes things work when it is present and makes things fall apart when it's not. Whether you are referring to an individual - such as your boss, a leader - or a group, a team, an entity - such as your company - your wish is to have it. It is difficult to be indifferent to the lack of it.

Trust is productive, it is full of consequences. Trust allows you to lower your defences because the level of threat goes down. You don't have to be on the alert all the time, like in aggressive and paranoid environments. In fact, in those environments, trust tends to calm things down and relieve tension. Trust also tends to generate loyalty. Since trust depends in part on visible transactions and behaviours of people, transparency increases with trust. Trust also triggers and fosters collaboration. It makes you freer and people will tend to engage more with others. It generates social capital, defined as the quality and quantity of the relationships among people. Other healthy organizational effectiveness processes such as delegation and empowerment are also largely dependent on trust. Reciprocity - a well-established psychological mechanism of value interchange between individuals (superficially: *"I'll do for you, you'll do for me"*) - is linked to trust like the chicken is to the egg. In particular, the so-called 'delayed reciprocity' (for example, "*I trust you, I know you'll do something for me in future when I need you to*") is well connected to trust.

My favourite characteristic - from the dozens of angles that research in this area has given us - is the effect that trust has in dealing with uncertainty. In a high trust environment, uncertainty doesn't disappear but it is more manageable, less threatening. Therefore, it increases the chances for us of looking at uncertainty as an opportunity, as a variety of possibilities, instead of as hostility and threats. It transforms victims into actors. And our business environment could do with a bit less victimization.

So leaders have a great duty to create and maintain trust, and what they 'do' is crucial for the success. If you have followed me on this psychosocial promenade, you will probably have added new - your own - characteristics of trust as we went along. We have all experienced the pleasure that trust gives us and the almost sadness that comes with the lack of it or its breakdown. Organizations and their individuals share quite a lot of the characteristics of trust, although we often seem to be happy to make a distinction: "*I don't trust the company, but I trust my manager or that leader*". Since trust - as described above - allows us to be more vulnerable without expecting negative consequences, our disappointment – when we do feel or are confronted with these negatives - triggers a possibly disproportioned reaction of the kind: "*I don't trust you anymore*". Trust seems to follow a possibly unfair 'all or nothing' rule. The breach of trust forces us to defend ourselves even with no immediate present threat. It is a sort of "*I will protect myself just in case, so, you are out*".

One of the most powerful ways for leaders to breach trust is to behave inconsistently with promises or verbalizations. Leaders who 'don't walk the talk' can usually not be trusted or, if they were trusted before, the visible incongruent behaviour destroys the trust-capital very quickly. Similarly, leaders' overt behaviours are the most powerful mechanism to create trust, well above the simple appeal: *"Trust me because I believe in X or Y"*. What you do or don't do as a leader has a lot of power in the building or destroying of trust.

Over history, some professions have gained quite a lot of collective trust-capital: i.e. doctors, the police and teachers. Periodical trans-cultural surveys are rather consistent about that. Politicians and business managers rank extremely low in the West. Amongst industries, pharmaceuticals rank very low in public trust, at levels similar to the tobacco and oil industry. It is generally well acknowledged that the pharmaceutical industry has a steep curve ahead to re-build (social) trust.

This industry is fascinating because it hosts the best intellectual capital in life sciences and because over the years it has developed the highest percentage of medicines, as compared with government or academia. One has to be suffering from social blindness to believe otherwise. Its societal relevance is unquestionable. However, year after year, the percentage of people who believe that the pharmaceutical industry is working for the public good never reaches 5%, whilst the percentage who thinks that it is all about profits – and very high profits at that - is always in the 70s or 80s.

In the last couple of years, we have seen a significant increase in 'initiatives' from companies within the drug industry to improve their image and hopefully rebuild trust. Many of them relate to territories such as drug safety, transparency of systems and most recently transparency of drug clinical trials results. The trust erosion is so bad that any serious philanthropic gesture or initiative in areas such as free or generous availability of essential drugs in developing countries (and there are dozens of these pharmaceutical industry examples) is immediately received with a certain dose of cynicism, simply not believed and certainly clouded by the bad image and reputation. Paradoxically, these 'positive social behaviours' may potentially be more powerful than all pharma CEOs together praising the achievements in tackling diseases and creating wellbeing.

▶ *"Don't worry about your image, but about your actions!"*

At a recent global pharmaceutical conference in London, one of the speakers - director of one the divisions of the World Health Organization - repeated the following advice several times: *"Don't worry about your image, but about your actions"*. In other words, only visible actions will restore trust and reputation. Not surprisingly, in his mind, those actions should be focused on dealing with HIV/AIDS and pandemic influenza, together with the re-diversion of marketing money to R&D, particularly for 'essential medicines'. The position of this public-health-civil-servant – which was met with different degrees of enthusiasm from the audience - was predictable. Whether pharmaceutical executives present agreed with his prescriptions or not, he had a point from the angle of the behavioural sciences of trust: the only hope is action, not linguistics. Leaders in any industry would gain a lot from studying the psycho-sociology of trust with care, as opposed to banking on PR or 'educational campaigns' only!

Still using the example of the pharmaceutical industry, many companies have some sort of socio-educational programme with the intention to educate the public on the merits of the drug industry. The big ones even have dedicated senior management for the topic. I have seen some of those programmes and, maybe it was bad luck, but I have never been impressed. They are all about telling people that the pharmaceutical industry has done this and that, that drugs make people better and cure diseases and that the drug industry cares about quality of life and wellbeing. They usually follow the PR model of 'listen to me' which has a very limited effect in terms of trust building. Unfortunately, it only takes a few 'bad examples' on the front page of newspapers to neutralize the 'educational efforts'. Logical argumentation meets emotional brain, *"How can we trust them if this and that happened?"*

Leaders build trust through actions wrapped up in emotional appeals. Trust - whether in politics, people, organizations, business management or reputation building - is probably the most important issue today. The Jewish jewellers in New York send diamonds to each other across the city in an envelope. Trust me, we need a dose of this.

Change

Another way I tend to answer the question, *"What do leaders do?"* - running the usual risk of big statement/ simplification - is by saying they constantly challenge the default position. Last time you bought a computer or a laptop, chances are it came with a ready-to-use software package. You appreciated that very much because you didn't have to load discs like in the old days. Your software allowed you to work straight away. It gave you a good feeling of mastering the stuff, you were proficient and you boasted to your teenage daughter that you knew how to work out these machines after all.

What you got that day in a box was your default system. Up and running, ready to go, not pretending to do anything but the minimum so that you could start working right away. Each application, however, had the built-in possibility of adjusting its settings and converting it into a more sophisticated one. In many cases, indeed, if you wished to, you could get very sophisticated, because the degree of potential customization was enormous. Once customized to your preferences, the new application looked very different from the default. It became 'yours'. But sometimes in the past, you chose not to customize and carried on with your default for a long time. You did not see anything wrong with that. After all, it had worked as it was. Even upgrades came along and you did not bother to use them. You had neither the time nor the energy to switch to another more complex version and, besides – you may have thought – who knew how the new one was going to work. Then, only a while later, your company decided to upgrade or change software altogether. Hey, that was a massive disruption, even if you were hand-held by the IT folks. At that time, you had no choice, somebody had chosen for you. So you moved to the next level.

▶ *Leading by default*

You may find this story more or less familiar, but you may not see how it relates to the world outside laptops and spreadsheets. However, organizations behave in the same way. You have your 'default organization': the one that is 'there', perhaps the one you have inherited after a merger or acquisition. And you may not hesitate to say "*it works*", nothing wrong with it. You join it day after day at nine a.m. on the dot and it takes you through to five pm with some ups and downs, but more or less safely. It is comfortable. It contains all you need. It has people performing tasks, managers supervising people and bosses managing the supervisors. It is OK, not sexy but OK. You can't ask for much more, certainly it would not lead to a lot of excitement and there is not much hope that it may generate a breakthrough. It is a good 'default organization' and you don't see anything wrong with it.

In bad times, things are different: people become stretched, supervisors become nervous, managers become restless (and start polishing their CVs). You, as leader of the company or the group, are now asking extraordinary efforts that need extraordinary systems, extraordinary people, extraordinary processes and extraordinary ideas. You don't have them. You have (created? led?) a default organization that was supposed to take you smoothly from nine to five – and so it only did just that.

Organizations that remain 'in default position' are unsuitable for times where a 'high customization' is needed. They simply can't cope. As Shakespeare put it, *"When the sea was calm, all ships alike showed mastership in floating"*[18]. I wonder whether Shakespeare was referring to organizational development. Mastership in running a 'floating organization for calm days' is like driving a car below 40 miles per hour with nobody on the road on a clear day. If this is what you do every day, you will have some difficulties racing in the Monte Carlo Grand Prix.

But many leaders seem happy with the default position, both for the organization and themselves. Indeed, 'default leadership' is widespread. These managers hold a MF qualification (Master in Floating). It's very handy for the good, clear, predictable and uneventful days in business life. Pity we are running out of such days fast.

▶ *Leading the inevitable*

Default leadership exhibits two types of behaviour or two characteristics. The first one could be called 'leading the inevitable', that is leading what will happen no matter what. Legions of managers spend their time managing plans and events that are going to happen anyway, instead of 'managing' what would not happen had they not been there. I have expressed this before in this book. Meetings after meetings, committees after committees, reviews after reviews and a ton of slides later something happens and leaders are

---

[18] Shakespeare, William, 1609, *The tragedy of Coriolanus*, Act 4, Scene 1

happy to correlate that event with the 'activity' of the meetings, the reviews and the 'presentations'. In a few cases, this is true. For the majority, the causality is no different from the one that could claim that since most of the inmates in prison smoked before they were jailed, criminality is caused by smoking. Many would laugh at such post-hoc fallacy, yet 90% of management is post-hoc fallacy management in a default environment.

In my previous career, working as a clinical psychiatrist, I had a patient, Carlos, who was a very bright paranoiac. Paranoia is a rare condition different from its cousin paranoid schizophrenia. Paranoiacs have a *single* mono-thematic delusion (false interpretation of a reality) which is impossible to change or modify by rational arguments. This very strong set of beliefs is the 'only' anomaly. There are no halluci-nations or other symptoms and the patient may otherwise have a 'normal' life (as long as the delusion does not interfere with others…). For example, a paranoiac may believe that he has invented the telegraph and explain this in detail. If the conversation does not come up or, indeed, as long as he does not decide to go and claim the royalties from the government, you may not notice anything wrong with this person. My patient Carlos was convinced that he had somewhat peculiar special powers. He used to travel by bus and was certain that he had the power to stop the bus every time it came to a red traffic light. Obviously, the bus stopped accordingly every time, not doing anything but reinforcing Carlos in his belief every single time.

I know many leaders who suffer from Carlos' Syndrome. They are convinced that what happens in the organization is the result of their endless meetings and reports, their fiddling with the organization chart and the Task Forces that they have set up to tackle issues. In many instances, things happen because their bosses had decided so a long ago, or the CEO has dictated that path, or simply because there was no other choice for that particular topic. They believe that all of it was due to their intervention and - like Carlos - they are positively reinforced by events. Because organizations don't take much time to do a good post-event analysis ('post mortem' or review of learning from the event) entire gene-rations of default managers and leaders are happy to live in their own delusional world, often taking their entire teams with them.

►Admiring the problems

The second behaviour that default leadership induces is what can be called 'admiring the problems'. Default managers and leaders may be good at diagnosis, but not at doing something about the problems. You have seen it before. Entire teams keep repeating, for example, *"We have a communication problem here."* But the daily repetition does not generate any action to fix it. 'Admiration of the problem' thrives in those environments and not surprisingly the self-fulfilling prophecy of the 'communication problem' takes over reality. They become paralysed by the label: the label is the reality. Whatever was happening in truth is irrelevant once people have articulated the label again and again, for example, the label 'communication problem'. It is the old nominalistic fallacy: name it (label it) and it exists.

Psychiatry, more than other branches of Medicine (but not a lot more!) has lots of these 'label admirations' and nominalistic fallacies. A mother brings a child who can't stand still, is constantly restless, cries for no reason, misbehaves, is unpredictable and, quite frankly, is quite unmanageable. Diagnosis: *"Madam, your son has emotional instability"* (what else could it be?!). Followed by the mother's, *"Aha! Now I understand"*. The apprehension of the label has decreased the anxiety of the uncertainty and as such is therapeutic – for the mother! But the concept refers simply to *the same* complex reality, now safely controlled by a two-word straight jacket.

Management labels are the same. The situation where people, groups, divisions are not talking well to each other, not passing information, working in silos, not sharing issues, not knowing what the other is doing, is labelled a 'communication problem' But there is no such a thing as a 'communication problem'. What it is, is …people, groups, divisions not talking well to each other, not passing information, working in silos, not sharing issues and not knowing what the other is doing.

Default managers admire problems but, even more, they admire their labels. And God knows there are plenty around. Leadership need to challenge the labels in order to understand the content and so do something about it!

► Challenging the default positions

John Searle, professor of Philosophy at Berkeley, defines philosophy as the challenge of the 'default positions' such as *"the existence of an external reality, the reality of personal consciousness, and the reasonable fit of language to the perceived world*"[19]. If unchallenged, these defaults become untouched. I'd like to suggest to you that leadership in organizations has to do with challenging the default organization. This is the one that does things 'the way they have always been done' and is organized in 'the way everybody is', etc.

The current business environment has no time for defaults, but still many organizations are based upon those. No wonder ships sunk a-la-16th Century-Spanish-Armada. It was also called the 'Invincible Armada'. This was a fleet intended to invade England and 'to put an end to the long series of English aggressions against the colonies and possessions of the Spanish Crown'. It was totally destroyed in a week by 'the weather'. After that, Spanish maritime power declined gradually. The Armada and Stalingrad have in common a battle against the wrong enemy: the weather. Similarly in business, we have our own Stalingrad and Armada: it's easy to blame the competition, the market volatility or political uncertainty. Taking a look at your own ships and your own clothing before going into battle would help.

Default leadership does not invent, default leadership does not build and default thinking will not lead to the next level of success for the organization and for its employees. As for the shareholders, they may still enjoy earnings per share according to expectations. Default organizations, after all, may meet stakeholders' expectations like the bus driver in Barcelona met Carlos' every single day.

---

[19] Searle, John R., 2000, *Mind, Language and Society: Philosophy in the Real World*, Basic Books, New York

There is no question that leading and driving change have blurred borders. So, could we explore this a bit more?

'We trained hard...but it seemed that every time we were beginning to form into teams, we would be reorganized. I was to learn later in life that we tend to meet any new situation by reorganizing, and a wonderful method it can be for creating the illusion of progress while producing confusion, inefficiency and demoralization".

This is not a quote from the latest biography of a retired CEO, or from a management consultant's book in an airport bookshop. It was written in 210 BC by Petronius Arbiter, who apparently had an insight or two into organizational development. In 513 BC, Heraclites observed that, *"There is nothing permanent except change."* And in the 16th century, Machiavelli stated in *The Prince, "There is nothing more difficult to take in hand, more perilous to conduct, or more uncertain in its success, than to take the lead in the introduction of a new order to things."* So, there you are – change and reorganization was sort of invented by the Roman army, had already been accepted as inevitable by the Greeks, and has continued ever since. But don't despair if you are part of it, even Machiavelli conceded that it is difficult. But, how difficult?

► *Resisting to change?*

If one has to judge this, using the conventional wisdom and shared beliefs in this area, the answer is very difficult. I can't think of any other phrase or statement more used in management conversations than the one that says *"People are resistant to change*". By repeating it like parrots, we have taken it at face value. If you heard somebody in a company saying that people are *not* resistant to change, your first impression would be that he, or she, must be nuts! Look around you: all these legions of consultants and academics saying the opposite; a whole industry of books, tapes, conferences and motivational speakers delivering 'how to' (change) solutions, all under the premise that people need to be pushed, otherwise they would prefer to remain static.

The Machiavelli school of change management is the official one: it's going to be difficult, pain is inevitable, people don't like it – push or else. There is a particular sector of the organization that has repeatedly been given the Oscar for the 'best resistance to change'. It's called middle management. Apparently, there is this layer in the organizational sandwich, somewhere in the middle, that blocks everything, resists everything and, quite frankly, that we would be better off without. So, that's what happened during the past two decades under the lean and mean corporate clean-up.

Hierarchical corporate structures became flat pancakes and those battalions of unhelpful managers in the middle – blockers of change, gatekeepers of information flow, obstructive individuals, corporate parasites and ugly people in the ranks of middle management – left big corporations to be resuscitated as top managers in smaller firms, enablers of change, providers of information and knowledge, facilitators of change, and beautiful consultants selling services to their ex-employers at a premium rate.

The science best positioned to understand corporate trans-formation and talent markets is not management science but ecology. The market place is an ecosystem of life and death, growth, maturity, degeneration, regeneration and, unlike biology, resuscitation. But this is a topic for another day. Now, suspend judgment for a minute, forget management and look around you. You may be married and have children who are small and growing, or already grown up and independent. You have perhaps moved jobs three or four times (if not more), moved house a couple of times, and perhaps emigrated a while ago. Look at your neighbours, they may be in a similar situation and, if not, surely you know others like you. As for your health, perhaps you feel a bit older now and have stopped doing the things that you did when you were younger, but you may have started doing new things that you didn't do until just a while ago. Perhaps you stopped smoking recently. Perhaps you have remarried and started a second family. If not, you know somebody who has. You may have seen your children going through primary and secondary school, abandoning you for university (and providing you with that spare room that you always wanted) and having boyfriends and girlfriends, who always look different from what you expected.

You've seen the death of your parents and the birth of your grandchildren, or you are now spending more time than ever with your surviving parents. When you look around, what you see is a symphony of change. People, emotions, attachments and geographies sometimes change with the rhythm of the seasons; at other times, with the violence of tsunamis and earthquakes. There is a name for all this: it's called life. In life, pain is inevitable but misery is a choice. I can't figure out who said this first – there are hundreds of people claiming authorship – but what I do know is that management could learn a thing or two here.

Just by looking at ourselves in the mirror we can see that all around us, and within ourselves, there is pure change. We are part of a Heraclites-type world where we constantly adapt. From a biological viewpoint, we are not resistant to change because we *are* change. You can't say that a baby resists becoming a child and the child resists becoming an adolescent. Life and change *are* the same word. There are different degrees of pain associated with the various changes but we are always in transition; we *are* transition. And, incidentally, the transformation from pain to misery is largely in our hands.

▶ *Change is inevitable, misery is a choice*

Sloppy, insensitive, mismanaged, unnecessarily prolonged change programmes in companies - whether on the back of a merger or an internal reorganization - create misery out of the possible pain. Creating unnecessary uncertainty by lack of clarity or openness produces anxiety that could evolve to unnecessary pain and misery. We are not talking here about the need for suppression of all forms of pain, but only the unnecessary hi-fi of pain. We all know that a deviant form of obtaining pleasure is to produce pain. We have a name for this: sadism. There are leaders who believe that part of their role is to turn up the pain hi-fi under their subordinates. That would apparently make them powerful. I know a few of those. They have a tremendous ability to create a sense of fear and misery around them!

So, what about change-cookbooks that can lead us to reasonable ends with some ingredients of pain, no misery and finally to a good dish on the table? There are hundreds of them, but for some reason John Kotter's – the legendary Harvard expert on leadership – are the ones quoted all the time. Kotter's steps for change read as: establishing a sense of urgency, creating a guiding coalition, developing a vision and strategy, communicating the change vision, empowering a broad base of people to take action, generating short-term wins, consolidating gains and, institutionalizing new approaches in the organizational culture. There you have it: follow the steps, add salt and pepper, put it in the oven, and change will be produced.

Far from dismissing or trivialising Kotter's approach, I think that it has the merit of making leaders feel that change is doable if certain conditions are created and some success factors are embedded. My main criticism is that there is too much sequence in this approach. Whether he supports this sequential view or whether it is the inevitable translation from the practitioner and reader's side, I don't know. After all, we are used to absorbing things such as the six steps from A to B, the five steps to become C, and the three steps for a successful D, etc. We are probably doing the same with managing change and Kotter's sequence makes sense in this context. But the biological reality - and therefore the psychological, psychosocial and leadership reality - is less sequential and more of a parallel nature.

The intense life of today's organizations, the pressure of challenges, the shortening of product and market lifecycles, the speed at which technology reinvents itself, the 24/7/365 knowledge of information and life, the ephemeral nature of many products and the compressed time and space that - whether you like it or not - characterizes business life today, forces us to look at things as 'whole systems' as opposed to as a 'sequence of events'. In plain English - and paraphrasing Woody Allen on London (*"all seasons in one afternoon"*) - we need the eight steps in one afternoon.

There is no such thing as a sequential, orderly business organization world, but there is a chaotic, multidimensional, network-centric, otherwise very rich one. Kotter's (and a Kotter-like) framework would work for me if we could establish a sense of urgency at the same time as creating a guiding coalition, and at the same time as developing a vision and strategy, communicating, empowering, generating wins, and consolidating gains, all in one and in parallel, all in the pot together and moving backwards and forwards. I know this is counterintuitive, but it's not impossible. I usually introduce behavioural change frameworks to my clients as a *"cultural change programme, and this is the last time you hear the word culture"*. Behaviours are what matters.

Talking about counter-intuition, people believe that cultural change is always slow, often painful and, on occasion, possibly miserable. This is true when it is not behavioural-focused. Putting the spotlight on behaviours has the advantage of producing faster-than-expected changes that, when properly reinforced, change the ways of doing things, which change culture 'without calling it a culture change'. The most popular change-management cookbook, Kotter's, is not behavioural and this is its main weakness. I accept that I may be the only management consultant alive daring to say this, and that it will sound to some like stating that the recipes of three-star Michelin restaurants are no good. But it is what I believe.

One key advantage of behavioural-focused change management is that it's fast and avoids misery. It doesn't get rid of pain, but it makes it very difficult to hi-fi it. Although Sun Tzu - in the 2,500-year-old *The Art Of War* - said that *"there is no invariable strategic advantage (shi), no invariable position (xing), which can be relied upon at all times"*, people in business are always looking for proven recipes, templates, repeatable process and standardised frameworks.

Practicing Seven Faces

This is a summary of summaries! What should leaders do? You won't be surprised at this stage of reading when I say that this question only has a personal answer, but that the consequences of your answer are not just personal! I need to go back to the beginning of this long conversation with you to refresh the premise of it and in doing so refresh the reason why I wrote it in the first place.

There are hundreds of theories and views on leadership. Some come from 'research', others are more experiential and intuitive. They all provide 'maps' as I referred to in a previous chapter. I have abandoned the theories and the list of qualities to launch questions. These are questions that I have put to myself in the past and continue to ask myself. I believe, as you know, that the leader has multiple faces, well, seven at least! And that we sometimes only see one or two of them.

We lead - leaders lead - using our own preferred default system, to use the term I have used above. But it doesn't mean that we are not capable of the other faces. We just take some of them for granted, or feel a bit uncomfortable or simply focus on the few things that we believe matter. I have mentioned before at the beginning of this book that just because a leader, for example, is very good at expressing things verbally, at articulating visions and sharing them with his people, he may not necessarily be good at thinking about his legacy, his succession or, say, the kind of place that his vision and articulations may be creating. Inversely, some leaders who rely much upon what they do and create in day-to-day life, may fail to articulate clearly where the organization is going or forget to invite people to follow. None of us is very good at everything!

The seven faces model is not a theory of leadership, it is a reminder that the only way to become better leaders is to practice it! And that we should do it across the seven dimensions and only presenting our own familiar face. 'Practicing the seven faces' means being active in all of them, not necessarily with a pristine balance between them but taking them all into account. So the following is not another theory, it is a summary of the key components of the seven faces as seen through my own glasses. It is as if you found me in the corridor, after a management team meeting, or a seminar or a long afternoon of working with you as consultant, and you asked me to give you my own personal view of leadership. In doing so, I am running a little bit the risk of reductionism. I am not suggesting for a second that you should take it at face value! Indeed, there are many other things that I have covered in this book that are not highlighted in the following paragraphs. But, now that we know each other a bit more, this is my own take of things. This is my dream profile. One that is difficult to reach, one that certainly I haven't reached myself and one that would stretch and challenge me. The sum of all would create a sort of Super-leader! Which is something of a caricature! But it doesn't mean that it is not achievable. Practice, practice and practice would take you and me 'there', without ever totally getting 'there' but... doing a pretty good job as leader-apprentices in the meantime!

1. My kind of leader asks lots of questions, provides answers when he thinks he has them and is able to say "*I don't know*" (followed by the perhaps occasional "*and I don't think you know either.*") He is not afraid of sharing that angle of vulnerability that comes from the 'I don't know', because it is always followed by the "*but we're going to find out, aren't we?*' My kind of leader provides a language. It is not necessarily a grandiose one and certainly not one full of jargon. But the aims are high, so the language is ambitious. It is a language of 'we' more than a language of 'I'. He tries to provide meaning to the organization. Sometimes he delivers hope through his language.

2. He says what he says in order to provide a common sense of purpose, to invite people to a shared commitment for action. He sometimes sounds like a teacher. He likes words not for the sake of them but as a 'glue for people' He is very aware that what he says matters. Practicing this face is about articulation, about 'translation' of the vision, about acknowledging that the most important leadership question is, "*what's the question?*" (that we have to address, that we need to solve and the answer to which will take us somewhere).

3. My kind of leader is a mapmaker. He acknowledges that there may be more than one way to reach the destination. Indeed, he may invite you to 'find that destination', running the risk of being seen as somebody who perhaps hasn't got total certainty about things. Certainly, he is not a destination-at-all-cost leader and cares about the multiple ways that people could travel. More than having a fixed idea of the destination, he is somebody who creates destinies. Both things are not the same. He is also a good traveller. He moves: forwards, backwards, sideways... but he is not static and certainly not in rehearsal mode waiting for better times to come. He travels with you and shares the pain: you use similar tight shoes, similar clothes and similar timetables. He also shares the good travel stops and celebrations. He looks and behaves like an explorer, a conquistador, a cartographer and a traveller.

4. My kind of leader is a builder. A builder of organizations, of ideas, of dreams, of 'houses'. Not physical houses but houses for 'space' and 'time'. He is somebody who creates the conditions for all to happen. He is a bit of a stage manager. Protecting 'time' and 'space' for people is not a New Age, soft, fuzzy, vague concept deprived of meaning. It is something very tangible that allows his followers to make the most of themselves in their own (personal) version of 'time to think', 'time to do', 'time for being'. As an architect, he cares not only about the management bricks-and-mortar in the organization but about what that edifice is going to host. He wants to host talent, human capital, relationships and, if he can,

unique competencies that no other 'house' may have! But he is also mindful about what will happen once he has departed either to… rest (?), build another house, or partner with another architect somewhere else. In other words, he takes his legacy very seriously. And he does so not in an arrogant way, but by making sure that the organization is not over-dependent on him and that it has become a great leadership school in itself.

5. My kind of leader has values. Like many other people! That in itself would not qualify him as my kind of leader! Not only does he have values, he is very focused on discovering other people's values and, in terms of the organization, 'uncover' the ones that may be hidden and non-articulated. He does not have a perfect answer to the potential conflict of values that daily business and organizational life sometimes bring to the table, but he is very aware of the potential 'corrosion of character' and would do anything to avoid it and would certainly not induce it in others. Sticking to values is important for him, so he has no problems with referring to them all the time, running the risk of being seen as a bit repetitive! One of the things he is certainly determined about, is not to let 'the system' be an excuse for abdicating responsibility. Although he cares a lot about 'the culture', 'our culture' or 'our way of life', he is not prepared to accept these - neither for himself, nor for his followers - as a justification for any action. For him, there are only non-negotiable behaviours (coming from non-negotiable values). If 'the culture' becomes an umbrella justification for poor leadership, he would ban the use of the word! On a personal basis, he will

never use the argument of 'sincerity' and 'authenticity' to justify his actions. He doesn't want history to judge him; he puts himself to the test of judgement in the day-to-day life of the organization.

6. My kind of leader uses measurements of success but measurements don't lead him or the organization. He is not a 'prisoner of the numbers' and, as a matter of fact, his discourse is not terribly full of them! He is good as a broker and - in practicing this - he is sometimes a bit in the background of things, letting others take the limelight. He is very conscious that sometimes 'the way we do things' kills good ideas and good processes and certainly could kill loyalty from people. His style of leadership is mainly one of moving forward. The occasional look in the rear view mirror of benchmarking doesn't feature as one of the core ingredients for the direction of the organization. Of course, he uses that data but he also uses judgement and other people's judgement. He really thinks that 'benchmarking is a race against somebody who has already won'. Speaking of which, he doesn't have a clear answer as to whether the organization should look like 'random joggers', 'a pack' or 'a race' or combinations thereof. But he is really aware of the concept of pace. He likes a sense of urgency but he doesn't always translate it as fast-at-all-cost. As a matter of fact, he finds that question of the 'pace' one of the most difficult ones. How to accommodate for different rhythms in people, for different tempos? He wishes he could have a formula to allow the fast marathoners to run without anybody else feeling guilty and, at the same time, not fall in the trap of

'organizational average' that works on a common denominator. He is still looking for answers here!

7. My kind of leader is cultivating emotional and social intelligence big time! It didn't come naturally. They had to be nurtured. He is still working on finding ways to grow in terms of awareness of himself, particularly of his own positive and negative influence. He cultivates an environment where awareness is very high on the agenda. Whether it is market, competition, own culture, mechanisms of conflict within his organization, etc, awareness is promoted. Awareness, for him, translates more like 'reflection' and 'judgement', than as myriad of market research data or employee surveys. He wants to understand the 'behavioural fabric' of the organization and wants his team and his followers to do the same. Far from avoiding 'the emotional side of things', he is bringing the emotions to the table in order to gain further advantage for the organization. He is also very aware of his responsibilities and accountabilities. The former he shares, the latter he keeps to himself.

8. My kind of leader is one who takes role modelling very seriously. He is not obsessed with the topic, and does not look into the rear view mirror all the time! But he certainly cares about the sync between 'his video and his audio'. What he says and what he does are consistent. He 'walks the talk' or at least this is his desire. He may not always get it right but he is certainly well aware of the enormous risks if he doesn't try. He wants to match values and behaviours. He thinks that by doing so, he will provide a

'reference' for others, a source of imitation that will be good for the organization. He makes a point that his immediate team does the same and has invested some energy, time and resources to take his team through a series of exercises to understand how good they are as leaders, what behaviours they exhibit, and, as he puts it, whether people would think it is worth following them! He is very conscious of the ephemeral and delicate condition of trust. Although he finds it very difficult to cater for every single possibility of trust erosion, he makes the point of behaving and leading with consistency, clarity and transparency so that he is not a source of that erosion. He does not buy in to the idea of a planetarian pandemic of 'resistance to change', but understands that this is a sort of expectation in the collective language! One of the ways he drives change is to simply challenge any default position in the organization. He clearly professes the belief that although change is sometimes painful, misery would be only his/their own choice.

Questions

- Use the list below to trigger new questions or to attempt to answer them! Make notes, use the book!
- Commit to one single step to 'answer the question'. These steps may look like actions you want to take, questions you want to ask other people in your organization or 'practice' that you want to do at your next opportunity.

Role Models

- Are you aware of any 'passive imitations' that your leadership may be producing?
- Are you aware of the real visibility of what you do, and the possible influence of your (leadership) actions?
- How do you create trust? Have you thought about that? Do you have any insight from others?
- How would you describe your organization, your close working environment in terms of trust?
- Could you have any influence on improving it?
- Is it worth it? Is it possible?
- How 'vulnerable' do you allow yourself to be seen by the people around you or working for you?
- Could you infer levels of trust from this?
- Do you consider yourself as somebody who 'walks the talk'?
- Would you consider situations in which you as a leader would say and do some things differently? Has it happened to you in the past?

Change

- Do you as leader challenge 'default positions'? Could you think of examples?
- Do you 'lead by default'?
- Do you think you are creating/leading an organization for extraordinary times or for calm seas?
- How much of your daily leadership is 'leading the inevitable'?
- How much of your effort is used in leading what would not happen if you were not there?
- Do you or your organization behave in the 'admiring the problem' mode?
- Do you consider yourself a change agent, change driver?
- Do you feel comfortable in this area as a leader?
- What's your position in terms of how painful change should be?
- Have you as a leader perhaps created unnecessary uncertainty in situations of change?
- How do you deal with the anxiety created around change whether for yourself or for others?

ACTION MAP
(some first pass questions)

Me   My organization

Me

Questions:
Do I see myself as a role model? Do I lead to create change?

Questions:
Do I generate trust? Do I 'walk the talk'? What behaviours of mine have a direct influence on the organization, possibly by 'passive imitation'?

My organization

Questions:
What behaviours do people around me see? What's the impact on them?

Questions:
What's our own role model capacity for people or for other groups? What's our collective readiness for change? How good are we at managing change?

This is a very simple set of questions to get you started with your reflections and actions. Use the blank pages to record your own questions and notes

▶ *Your Questions and Notes:*

▶ *Your Questions and Notes:*

The Leader with Seven Faces

Epilogue
Five acid tests of collective leadership

A few years ago, I was invited to talk to a newly created corporate team in one of the top 10 pharmaceutical companies. In fact, it wasn't totally new. It had been created a few months before as an amalgamation of some functions. But it felt pretty new to the rest of the company, since not many people seemed to know what that group was about. It didn't help that it had been created in the way the top leader of the organization - let's call him Joe - liked to create things: launching the concept and leaving the rest of the mortals to figure out what it meant in practical terms.

After a few months of soul-searching, dozens of brainstorms and the production of new business cards, the team reached the climax represented by the existence of a mission and vision statements. And I, as an external organizational consultant, was the one to receive the good news at the next meeting. I was supposed to comment and advise on the development of the small management team. The presentation followed the standard PowerPoint attack. It was pleasant, passionate, potent and predictable. Particularly the latter, since the mission statement was undistinguishable from any other mission statement of any other corporate group I knew.

Initially, I upset them a lot - and I still regret it today - by suggesting that if a secretary had mistakenly changed the title of the team and written next door's division instead, the mission would still hold. What surely proved that the mission didn't say anything about the uniqueness of the team.

Once we had de-dramatized the situation (allowed ourselves some non-threatening laughs), I revealed to them the risky strategy of 'going back to basics'. I asked them whether they could answer a simple question, as a team: *"Why are you here?"* Of course they could, no problem. To help the corporation to be successful. To improve shareholder value. To support the development of new products. And a dozen or so more reasons. *"May I give you my thoughts?"* I said. *"I think you are here because Joe said so."* By that time, we were all used to some laughs together and we developed the rest of the day with more plain English and less maximization of shareholder value. That was the good news. The bad news was they had to go way back to zero base.

There are many groups like this in corporations, more than you may think. They are not teams; they are groupings, juxtapositions of individuals who have landed together through the design of an organizational structure, the commonality of a task, the membership of a project or the far more prosaic reason of all: the fact that they are all direct reports of somebody. The first task of such groups is to recognize that they may not be a team yet. They will probably progress towards constituting one. That progression may be fast or slow, smooth or bumpy, exciting or forgettable.

In the case of leadership teams of any sort - whether corporate or divisional, business or NGOs, private or public - they are probably going to be rather visible. At some point in their life cycle, others are going to make judgements: are they a good team, or a bad team, or not a team at all?

People are going to make such judgements based upon a few facts and lots of perceptions. That's life. The management team may have reached some maturity after some time, they may function reasonably well, they may be successful, efficient, respected. Their output may be very visible in terms of decisions, resource allocations, communications to employees, roll-outs of business plans, review processes, pristine performance appraisals. Not bad. Is this quasi-perfect machinery a good representation of collective leadership? Not necessarily. A bicycle is perfect machinery. They may be proficient bike riders. The issue is whether they should be Ferrari drivers.

► *The leadership tipping point*

A good leadership team - a blessing in its own right for the organization - is not a true leadership team until they reach a tipping point at which the efficiency of the machinery becomes a pass, a baseline. At some point, some leadership teams throw away the bikes and start looking for the real thing. For whatever mechanism (or combination of mechanisms) they have, they reach a higher level of complexity at which the bike riders are able to see possibilities they could not see before.

There is a wealth of ideas on how teams at the top progress, how they become dysfunctional or high performance, how they excel or die. If you work in any organization today -

unless you have been on secondment to Mars for a while - you will probably have come across a model of some sort that explains how teams become good, or great or super-great. You may work in a corporation where there are declared values and beliefs, officially desired qualities of leadership or even a formal internal leadership development programme. The repertoire of desired characteristics of management teams - or the top leadership team in your organization - may read something like this (I have copied, pasted and edited one of multiple 'models'):

"We profess participative leadership by creating an interdependence by empowering, freeing up and serving others. We believe in shared responsibility; that is, establishing an environment in which all team members feel responsibility for the performance team as the manager. We are aligned on the purpose why the team exists and the function it serves. We profess high communication by creating a climate of trust and open, honest communication. We are future-focused: we see change as an opportunity for growth. We are focused on task; we keep meetings and interactions focused on results. We support individual talents and creativity. We are action-driven; we profess rapid response by identifying and acting on opportunities."

Oh boy, that sounds good. However, how do I know that a particular high performance leadership team - which is possibly doing well in most of the above (in whatever forms of specific translation to the needs of a particular organization) - has truly reached a level of leadership, Ferrari-style? Or, same question in a different way: how do I know whether they have only sophisticated the bike or whether they are riding the real thing? In the past, many people have asked me which organizational model I use, which leadership development framework I follow, what management theory or what leadership tribe I belong to. Or simply, at which point am I willing to crown a group a leadership team? Let me share the answer with you: I have five acid tests, which form my very sophisticated score system. You are allowed to fail one test out of five.

1. The ex-directory test

Without referring to the intranet, the internal telephone book or that HR binder on the shelf, could you name the members of that leadership team? For years, I have been bemused by the lack of recognition of names of a given leadership team by sometimes no more than two or three levels below the members. In the case of a big multinational – with classical multi-sites - I consulted for, a rather senior person-cum-big-salary could not name the composition of her boss' boss leadership team, which was the top divisional leadership one. I then discovered that this was not uncommon at middle management level. They used to explain the phenomenon with arguments such as *"They change all the time"* (which in that case was certainly not the case) or *"Well, I don't see them, they are across the Atlantic"*, etc. It is impossible for me to accept (hence my acid test) that a leadership team can not be named by people, but still be a good leadership team. I do not necessarily blame the ones who can't tell (although it is a bit pathetic), but the leadership team itself. They may be at the top, but with lots of cloud cover. It tends to indicate that they have not come down from their mountain that often.

OK, I'll give you a clue here. I said you could fail one test, but didn't say which one. Well, this is the only one you can fail because it relies on external validation. And I am willing to concede that occasionally the entire organization may be blind! However, the next remaining four tests are non-negotiable; they have to do with internal dynamics of the team. You fail one of those and I won't give you the leadership Ferrari label, no matter how many bikes you have in store.

2. **The 'can-I-help-you' test.**
True leadership team members systematically practice a spontaneous *"Can I help you?"* with the rest of the members. Some people may experience problems, a crisis, a sudden resource constraint and others jump spontaneously, *"How can I help you?"* Why am I making a fuss of this, to the point of elevating it to the category of acid test? The majority of leadership teams - particularly at top level in any organization of some size - are composed by functional representation. The team is very often composed of the directors of function A, B, C, D, plus, perhaps, the HR, Finance and IT directors (often called 'support functions'). They all have their worries, their constraints, their shops to look after. By definition, they are also very different in their functional expertise. Common wisdom says that the Finance director, for example, is unlikely to be able to 'help' the Director of, say, Regulatory Affairs or Engineering in R&D. This is so embedded in the system that even in high performance super-bike teams it would be simply unexpected. Which prompts the finance director to switch off in terms of 'jumping to help', creating a self-fulfilling prophecy. However, there are lots of areas where intelligent senior

people can help each other regardless the functional expertise. If spontaneous *"can I help you?"* dynamics are not present beyond the excuse *"but I don't know anything about that"*, you don't pass my test. I know that this may not necessarily have an impact on your sleep pattern, but well ... that's your prerogative.

3. **The commons test**

The well-known 'Tragedy of the commons' metaphor – which I also referred to in the 'How you do it' face - tells us that if all the herdsmen bringing cattle to the common pasture ('the commons') do so in their own interest - maximizing the utility (for them individually) of adding one more and one more - then at some point there will be no pasture left for anybody. Actually, it is in each of the herdsmen's best interest to refrain from adding cattle. *"If not"*, the author says, *"therein is the tragedy: each man is locked into a system that compels him to increase his herd without limit, in a world that is limited. Ruin is the destination toward which all men rush, each pursuing his own best interest in a society that believes in the freedom of the commons. Freedom of the commons brings ruin to all"*. Amen.

In a sense, a top leadership team is managing their 'commons'; that is, a finite set of resources. My acid test is passed if the members of the leadership team - probably representing different lines or functions - have a 'commons' approach and would spontaneously share, for example, headcount, even if transitorily. The keyword here is *spontaneously*. They do not need the dictation from the top boss. It is the way they do things: my commons are your commons.

4. The 'one hat' test

Very early in the progression of the maturity curve of the team, the issue of what hat to wear would have come up. In a pre-leadership stage, members wear one hat only: their own (i.e. the one reflecting whatever the job description says they have to represent). After all, that is why and how they got there in the first place. Very soon, people will be confronted with the idea of wearing another hat as well: the team hat. So, now, they have two hats: the functional one (as in the job description) and the leadership team one. This is not bad. There will probably be the usual explicit or implicit discussions about which one is bigger or more important and they may even settle for a courageous 50/50. But this is still good bike riding leadership. Members of a true leadership team that passes my acid test wear only one hat, and that is the leadership team one. And that hat includes everything else.

So the progression is one hat, two hats, and back to one hat again. Their functional and managerial responsibilities are a given, a baseline (hat one). The double hat (functional + leadership team) represents a good stage of development; one that many so-called leadership teams fail to achieve. But it's a good stage. However, the next step is a back-to-one-hat-leadership, where members of the team elevate themselves above their functional role and above the dual-hat-functioning-well-team to…well, to just lead the organization! Outside the team meeting, for example, they will wear whatever hat their payslip says they wear, but in the leadership team - acid test passed - there is only one hat to wear.

The secondary or surrogate acid test is whether they have created some (at least initial) *confusion* in the troops by presenting or communicating on topics that are not their area of expertise. No confusion, bad. Confusion: that's good. Because people do not expect a Finance Director to present the new pipeline (on behalf of the leadership team) or a Government Affairs director presenting the overall budget.

5. **The absent seat test**
   If one of the leadership team members is suddenly called upon to lead an urgent all-time-consuming project; or if the top leader needs to manage a corporate crisis which will take him 'away' for a while; one thing happens in a true leadership team passing my last acid test. There is an immediate *spontaneous* temporary reallocation of responsibilities making the 'absence' very invisible. The team is de facto functioning as true leadership team with one or more fewer members, but with no damage. Particularly important: when the man at the top can disappear for periods at a time and the leadership team behind him continues as normal - with the necessary adjustments but in full blown action mode - then you can say that true leadership is there. It is not a question of pushing the envelop by suggesting that the top leader should be made redundant as the ultimate test. Because I actually don't buy this. But the invisibility and inconsequential nature of the absence is a key sign of collective leadership.
   You could try these acid tests with your own leadership team and see what happens. If your answer is, *"We are here because we report to Joe"*... well, on your bike until you find the Ferrari dealer.

This book has mainly focused on the individual aspects of leadership. Only in this epilogue have I begun to address the collective leadership: starting with acid tests but without discussing how to get there. Well, I guess that's for our next conversation.

Thanks for reaching this point with me. One last thing to say: keep moving!

About the Author

Leandro Herrero practised as a psychiatrist for more than fifteen years before taking up senior management positions in several pharmaceutical companies, both in the UK and the US. He is co-founder and CEO of The Chalfont Project Ltd, an international firm of organizational consultants. Taking advantage of his behavioural sciences background - coupled with his hands-on business experience - he works with organizations of many kinds on structural and behavioural change, leadership and human collaboration.

Index

A

accountability, 115, 117, 210, 232, 257, 258, 265, 299
admiring the problems, 284
alliances, 123
associability, 128, 131, 136
assumptions, 59, 61, 62, 242, 244, 246
attitude surveys, 243
authority, 42, 48, 145, 153, 159, 210, 233, 234, 252, 262, 263
awareness, 11, 108, 232, 233, 255, 256, 264, 299

B

behavioural
  behavioural DNA, 216, 244
  behavioural economics, 63, 275
  behavioural sciences, 64, 66, 75, 153, 249, 250, 279, 317
beliefs, 10, 12, 132, 143, 144, 169, 172, 173, 207, 222, 235, 239, 245, 256, 283, 287, 310, 324
belonging, 11, 96, 118, 136, 160, 232, 260, 261, 262, 265
benchmarking, 197, 198, 200, 203
best practices, 198, 201, 202, 223
boundaries, 115, 116, 118
broken windows, 247, 248, 249, 251, 252, 253, 254, 255
broker, 212, 214, 224, 298
  brokerage, 117
  brokerage skills, 213, 214
  organizational broker, 212
bullet-pointing, 46
Business schools
  Business, 2

C

can I help you?, 312
change, 145, 271, 280, 290, 302
  change management, 87, 201, 207, 288
chaos, 126
character, 147, 150, 173, 262, 297
charisma, 1, 5, 40
coalitions, 43
collaboration, 123
  collaboration by design, 127, 136
commitment, 41, 47, 101, 102, 127, 133, 186, 197, 295
common purpose, 41, 112
complexity theory, 124
compliance, 252, 253
confidence, 4, 181, 236
conformity, 159, 273
consultation, 43
contingent, 161, 162, 170, 174
co-opetition, 123
corrosion of character, 143, 147
credos, 69, 87
culture, 10, 14, 114, 119, 135, 144, 154, 174, 187, 209, 221, 243, 257, 291, 292, 298, 299
customers, 30, 132, 183, 212, 214, 222, 246

D

decisions, 61, 62, 63, 113, 132, 170, 181, 196, 239, 244, 253, 258, 264, 309
default
  default leadership, 282, 286
  default organization, 281, 286
  position, 280, 282, 285, 300, 302
destinations, 56, 71, 87
destiny, 10, 26, 42, 45, 72, 102, 118, 262

S

scarcity, 43
self-help, 1, 27, 64, 65, 66, 67
self-managed teams, 127
shareholder, 130, 183, 222, 286
  shareholder value, 25, 33, 95,
    183, 205, 308
sincerity, 148, 173, 298
social capital, 96, 123, 127, 128,
  129, 130, 276
social intelligence, 240
social proof, 42
social Psychology, 158, 159, 160
space, 10, 96, 106, 108, 110, 135
  social space, 109
speak, 24, 45, 46
speed, 32, 105, 106, 119, 135, 217,
  218, 220, 291
stakeholder, 183, 214, 257, 286
stay interviews, 242, 243, 245, 246,
  247
strategic frameworks, 69
strategic intent, 44
structures, 182, 216, 224
styles, 182, 204, 223
  styles of leadership, 40, 222
succession, 133
synchronicity, 216, 217, 219, 220,
  224

T

talent, 95, 96, 106, 117, 120, 121,
  122, 133, 136, 256, 289, 297
targets, 26, 30, 70, 72, 78, 81, 130,
  145, 192, 219, 220
team spirity, 206
teamocracy, 124, 126, 130, 221
terra incognita, 72, 73, 87
test
  absent seat test, 315
  commons test, 313
  ex-directory test, 311
  teach-to-the-test, 191
the commons, 214, 215, 216, 224,
  313

tragedy of the commons, 215,
  313
time, 10, 96, 97, 101, 103, 105, 108,
  135, 145
  protection of time, 95, 106, 111
  time management, 97, 105, 111,
    252
  time-less leader, 103
translation, 5, 24, 29, 255, 291, 296,
  310
trial and error, 76
trust, 10, 11, 63, 72, 80, 117, 146,
  152, 153, 170, 207, 209, 233,
  274, 275, 276, 277, 278, 279,
  300, 301, 310
tyranny of the 'or', 32

U

uncertainty, 33, 39, 184, 235, 276,
  285, 286, 290, 302
uniforms, 63, 157, 159, 160, 161,
  174
uninspiring leaders, 14
universal scripts, 65, 67
Unspeak, 33, 34
urgency, 119

V

validity, 189
values, 12, 30, 64, 132, 133, 134,
  143, 144, 145, 146, 147, 148,
  149, 164, 169, 170, 171, 172,
  173, 174, 175, 209, 244, 256,
  297, 300, 310, 324
  dead values, 149, 174
  end-status values, 146
  living values, 149
  means-values, 146
  value system, 10, 143, 144, 161,
    170, 174, 181
venture
  internal ventures, 120
  joint-venture, 123

<meetingminds>

To order extra copies of *The Leader with Seven Faces*, visit our website at www.meetingminds.com. Also available to buy at www.amazon.com and at www.amazon.co.uk. For bulk orders, please contact us directly for more information on discounts and shipping costs.

Extended management tools: If you are interested in using *The Leader with Seven Faces* book as a **management or leadership development tool**, let us know. We may be able to provide you with extra documentation, associated reading lists, full reprints of related articles or other tools. There is also a workbook (available on demand): *The Leader with Seven Faces: workbook*. Please contact us for more information.

Customized editions: These are special editions created for a particular audience, such as a specific **company or organization**. The core materials of the book are maintained, but relevant company-specific resources - such as in-house case studies or tool-kits – are added. The text will also refer to internal frameworks such as your own values and beliefs systems, declared strategy, credo or other existing tools. A **special foreword** or tailored introduction - written either by the author or by your company's leadership - may be added as well. The book cover could also be adapted. Using modern printing technology, we can supply virtually any number of copies, from small runs to bulk production. If you are interested, please contact us.

Continue the conversation: Both a short seminar and a full leadership programme by Leandro Herrero are available. Details can be obtained via www.thechalfontproject.com, through which you can also contact the author.

<meetingminds>
Meetingminds publishing
PO Box 1192, Beaconsfield, HP9 1YQ, United Kingdom
Tel. +44 (0)208 123 8910 - **www.meetingminds.com**
info@meetingminds.com

Lightning Source UK Ltd.
Milton Keynes UK
UKOW02f1315290516

275148UK00001B/85/P

9 781905 776009